JUNIOR LEADER
HANDBOOK

JUNIOR LEADER
HANDBOOK

BOY SCOUTS OF AMERICA

33500A
ISBN 0-8395-3500-7
©1990 Boy Scouts of America
Revised 2000

Contents

It's Official—You're a Leader!

How does it feel to be called a leader? Pretty great, right? A real trip? For sure. Scout's honor now, it feels a little scary too, doesn't it?

Well, don't worry. You're in good company. Most everyone who has the chance to be a leader feels the same way. You have every right to be proud, happy, and a little scared. Remember, you're not the first person to get a new job. And you're not the first to ask yourself, "What do I do now?" That's what this book is all about.

We're going to take a good look at each junior leader position in Scouting and show you what's involved. You've probably already realized that your new job is more than just an honor. It's a challenge.

You're *officially* a leader. Whether you were elected or appointed to your new position as a junior leader, you'll be expected to shoulder some pretty heavy responsibilities. Others in your patrol and troop are expecting you to make a difference, and you will.

❑ You'll lead your patrol and troop at meetings and other activities.

- [ ] You'll help decide the course your patrol and troop will travel along the Scouting trail.

- [ ] You'll help other Scouts master Scouting skills.

- [ ] You'll be a role model for other Scouts. Your example will show them what being a Scout is all about. This is possibly your most important responsibility.

What Is Leading Anyway?

Leading is one of those challenges that can be defined in countless ways. For our purposes here, think of it this way. A leader is expected to get others to work together.

A real leader uses teamwork and respect for others to get the job done. If others think of you as the boss, you're probably not leading. If they think of you as one of the guys *and* everything you set out to do is getting done, you can bet you're doing a pretty good job of leading.

This handbook will help you discover ways to lead that make it almost easy—definitely fun!

Your Scoutmaster and assistant Scoutmasters already use the same skills and techniques that you'll discover in these pages. Watch them closely. They ask a lot of questions and make many *suggestions*, don't they? They don't give too many *orders*.

Use them as a resource. When you face a new challenge, chances are they've faced the same or a similar challenge. They can help you meet the challenge.

Finally, it's important to see, right from the start, that thousands of Scouts have been down the trail you're just beginning to travel. You can take advantage of their experiences. One of the easiest ways to do this is through junior leader training.

This is a *must*. It will help you discover what's expected of a leader in your position. When you know how to be right, it's a lot easier to be right. The more often you can do the right things, the more the other Scouts—and people in general—will respect your leadership.

Your Scoutmaster and assistant Scoutmasters already use the same skills you'll acquire as a junior leader.

Shortly now, your Scoutmaster will conduct an introduction to leadership. This brief training session, along with this *Junior Leader Handbook* will get you started. Then you're in for a real treat when you attend the troop junior leader training conducted by your Scoutmaster and senior patrol leader. After completing this course, you can wear the "trained" emblem for your new leadership position. Later on, once you have some experience in a leadership position, you'll want to get into a weeklong training conference conducted by your BSA local council. You may even look forward to participating in the National Junior Leader Instructor Camp held each year at Philmont Scout Ranch in New Mexico.

Leaders, Leaders Everywhere

There are many exciting and challenging positions for junior leaders in Scouting. While Scouts are frequently introduced to leadership through "assistant" positions, we're going to concentrate on the key positions: patrol leader, scribe, quartermaster, senior patrol leader, troop guide, Order of the Arrow troop representative, junior assistant Scoutmaster, librarian/historian, instructor, and chaplain aide.

Take a look at the names for these positions. They pretty much tell what the job is about. A patrol leader leads his patrol, the senior patrol leader leads the troop, and so on. It's easy to see that the "assistant" in each of these roles will get some experience leading the patrol or the troop when he fills in.

Get into Your Job

So you have to get into your new job right now. Perhaps you're a new patrol leader who has to plan for a weekend camping trip. You might be the new senior patrol leader looking forward to your first patrol leaders' council meeting. As a newly appointed troop quartermaster, you could be faced with a troop supply room that really wasn't put back the way it should have been after the troop returned from camp. It really doesn't matter. You've got a job to do, a job that looks as big as a mountain.

When you first set out to conquer your new job, it's quite natural to be a little concerned. It's easy to find yourself wondering, "How am I ever going to pull this off?"

Break It Down

When you've got a big job to do, it's a good idea to break it down into little pieces and tackle one piece at a time. It doesn't seem so big that way. Then start by doing the things you're most familiar with.

This book provides the tools you'll need to break down the jobs of a junior leader into smaller pieces so you can successfully attack your new challenge right away.

Think of your *Junior Leader Handbook* as a toolbox. Take it with you to meetings. Take it along on campouts, hikes, and, of course, to summer camp. This toolbox has all the basic tools you'll need to get the job done.

After you've used it for awhile, you may find that you don't refer to it as often because you've grown into your position as a junior leader. Still, on occasion you'll discover that a new challenge has jumped up and hit you between the eyes. Having your *Junior Leader Handbook* close at hand to refer to is a lot like having a toolbox with all the right tools for the job.

Still, there are times when a tool will be needed that is not in this toolbox. You will need to look somewhere else. The handbook will identify other "toolboxes" like the *Boy Scout Handbook*, and *Troop Program Resources*. Often the best help will come from one of your troop's adult leaders or another junior leader.

So, if you haven't already done it, fill in the nameplate in the front of this handbook. Then get ready. You're in for a real adventure.

Chapter  2

Standing Tall, Up Front

The Job of the Senior Patrol Leader

That's exactly where Tom, the senior patrol leader, found himself at the first troop meeting of the fall. He was a little nervous at first. After all, it was a new experience. The Scout room at the church was filled with the voices of friends getting ready to start a new adventure. High fives, backslapping, laughing, and joking filled the room at an almost deafening level. It wasn't unlike dozens of previous meetings except that it was Tom's first as senior patrol leader.

"Fall in," he announced in his best leadership voice. The Scouts quickly began to move into the traditional troop formation around the U.S. flag and troop flag. Some of the new guys were a little slow catching on to what was happening but the "veteran" Scouts took care of that in quick order.

Wow! The jitters were gone almost as fast as the words, "Fall in," fell out. The meeting was under way. There really wasn't time to be nervous any more.

Just as the patrol leaders' council had planned, the opening ceremony began. The U.S. flag and the troop flag were hardly back in their stands before Tom heard himself asking for patrol reports. Bob, the Fox patrol leader, stepped forward and began.

"Senior patrol leader, the Fox Patrol is all present and proud to announce . . ." Each patrol leader would have a

The senior patrol leader might take a minute to teach a skill during a troop meeting.

similar report. Before he knew it, the opening ceremony was over, the Scoutmaster had made a few announcements, and the meeting was in full swing. To an outsider it could have looked like total confusion.

Tim, the Fox Patrol's assistant patrol leader, walked across the room, looking at a piece of paper in his hand. He obviously was on a mission.

The Cobra Patrol ran out the door. They were getting ready for a demonstration on fire building.

The Roadrunner Patrol quartermaster was looking for the troop quartermaster. The Roadrunners were in charge of the interpatrol activity for the night's meeting and needed some supplies from the quartermaster store.

Tom handled each situation quickly and easily. Then he checked to see if the Scoutmaster was available for a Scoutmaster conference (that's what Tim's note was about).

A quick check with the Foxes made sure everything was in order for the closing ceremony. Then he visited briefly with the Roadrunners to answer questions about the next campout. Finally Tom was outside checking on the three skills demonstrations.

It was all in a night's work for a senior patrol leader. And it really wasn't too difficult. He was prepared.

Just Call the Senior Patrol Leader the Emcee

Let's take a look at what Tom was up to. The senior patrol leader is sort of the master of ceremonies, isn't he? He makes sure everything is happening the way it was planned. As senior patrol leader, Tom got the meeting started. While the patrols were going about their business, he was paying attention. If anyone needed help, he'd lend a hand or point out who could.

Looking Ahead

After Tom said goodnight to the patrol leaders, there was still a brief review meeting with the Scoutmaster and other adult leaders. Not until this meeting is over could he consider the troop meeting complete.

As you've already seen, the senior patrol leader really runs the troop meeting. It's important that he think ahead. The review session with the adult leaders is all about thinking ahead.

The Scoutmaster asks a bunch of questions. How did the patrol leaders' council's plan work out? Did advancement take place? Are the right things happening so that the troop will be ready for the next campout? What has to be done to get prepared for the next meeting? Did everyone have fun tonight?

When you first look at these questions, they look simple enough. Look again. How did the plan work? That's not an easy question. You might be tempted to just answer, "Fine." But that is not a good answer. You're going to want to be able to discuss how it worked. Before you answer a question like this, ask yourself a couple of other questions.

"What did I really like about the way the plan worked?" This question allows you to focus on those things that work well. You'll take notice of activities that everyone enjoyed. You'll recognize events that really had all the Scouts working together as patrols. You'll discover that the advancement you planned into the meeting actually took place.

The second question you'll want to ask yourself is, **"What would I like to do differently next time?"** This helps you "think positive." If you noticed that one patrol was having difficulty with a particular skill, then you might want to schedule some skill development activities for this patrol. If the opening ceremony was a little long, consider talking to the patrol leader responsible for the next ceremony about how important it is to be brief.

These questions help you concentrate on what went right (rather than on the problems) and what you're going to do to make it even better next time. The more you think about the right things you're doing or planning to do, the better.

Your Friend, the Scoutmaster

Before you became a senior patrol leader you probably noticed that the Scoutmaster and the senior patrol leader work together.

This is natural. The Scoutmaster depends on the senior patrol leader. The senior patrol leader needs the Scoutmaster as a friend and leader. This relationship is important because it's the foundation upon which the whole troop rests. In order to succeed as a senior patrol leader, you'll need to understand this.

Your Scoutmaster has been down the trail before. Your Scoutmaster has faced the problems and has met the challenges. Perhaps most important, though, is your Scoutmaster's knowledge of Scouting and the troop. This person was probably an assistant Scoutmaster before serving as Scoutmaster, so your Scoutmaster has learned from past adult leaders.

As a friend, your Scoutmaster will let you share some of this experience. A Scoutmaster will back you up when you face a particularly tough challenge and will be there when you need some support.

Look at your friend, the Scoutmaster, as a resource. Your Scoutmaster will have answers when you need them. If not, your Scoutmaster will help you find answers.

Helping Others Grow

The senior patrol leader doesn't get time off just because the event isn't a troop meeting. No, sir. He's in charge at all troop events and activities. On campouts, hikes, and service projects, at campfires, courts of honor, or district competitions, your job is to make certain everything is going as planned and that everyone is prepared to do his job.

When someone doesn't do the assigned task, it's the senior patrol leader who has to find someone who will. This isn't a matter of passing the buck. It's an important part of your job. You could easily do the assigned task yourself. But remember what we say to the patrol leaders in chapter 3. No one can do everything.

When someone drops the ball, you'll want to resist the urge to pick it up and run with it. Rather, pick it up and pass it to someone else. This is called delegating. A good leader will do a lot of delegating.

Delegating not only allows you to do other things, it also allows others to grow in their experience. The most natural one for the senior patrol leader to delegate to is the assistant senior patrol leader. After all, his job is to back up the senior patrol leader, filling in when you're not available.

Also, you already know from your experience as a patrol leader or assistant senior patrol leader, that you have other junior leaders you can depend on, too. You'll likely find yourself calling on the troop quartermaster, troop scribe, or perhaps even one of the patrol leaders without even thinking about it.

Don't try to do everything yourself—pass the ball to someone else.

Here's the job of the
in a nutshell:

SENIOR PATROL
LEADER

Job description: The senior patrol leader is elected by the
Scouts to represent them as the top junior leader in the troop.

Reports to: the Scoutmaster.

Senior patrol leader duties:

- ☐ Runs all troop meetings, events, activities, and the annual
  program planning conference
- ☐ Runs the patrol leaders' council meeting
- ☐ Appoints other troop junior leaders with the advice and
  counsel of the Scoutmaster
- ☐ Assigns duties and responsibilities to junior leaders
- ☐ Assists the Scoutmaster with junior leader training
- ☐ Sets a good example
- ☐ Enthusiastically wears the Scout uniform correctly
- ☐ Lives by the Scout Oath and Law
- ☐ Shows Scout spirit

The Senior Patrol Leader's Sidekick

The assistant senior patrol leader is like a best friend.
He's always there when he's needed. There is more to being
the assistant senior patrol leader than just waiting around
until someone needs your help, however.

If you really take the Scout motto, Be Prepared, to
heart, you'll have the job of the assistant senior patrol leader
well in hand. As assistant senior patrol leader, you should be
prepared to fill in for the senior patrol leader on a moment's
notice, or less.

What happens, for example, when the senior patrol
leader is working with the Fox Patrol on their closing

ceremony? Does everyone have to wait until he's done to get some attention? Definitely not, if the assistant senior patrol leader is really prepared.

The Senior Patrol Leader-Assistant Senior Patrol Leader Team

The cocaptain of a ball team doesn't sit on the sidelines waiting for the captain to tell him to carry the ball. Why should the assistant senior patrol leader wait around for direction from the senior patrol leader? Certainly there are times when he'll receive specific assignments. In between, though, he can play a key role in each meeting or activity if he pays attention and comes prepared.

On the way to the patrol leaders' council meeting, assistant senior patrol leader George and senior patrol leader Tom tossed a couple of high fives while discussing the weekend campout. They even joked about some of the glitches they'd noticed. They were already thinking about things that would make the next trip even better.

George had been in charge of the campfire and had some ideas for making it even more fun. Tom agreed, but he wanted to get one of the patrols involved, so he asked George to try his ideas while working with one of the patrols. At the patrol leaders' council meeting, they'd ask a patrol leader to volunteer his patrol to plan and conduct the campfire. The assistant senior patrol leader would be their coach.

At the patrol leaders' council planning table, George sat next to Tom. From here he could give Tom his ideas without interrupting the meeting. Also, just by paying attention, he would know what Tom was trying to accomplish, the decisions that were made, and why they were made.

Later, when Tom is involved with something else, George can step in easily and quickly. Because he paid attention, he will be prepared. He can act the way the senior patrol leader would act.

Here's the job of the in a nutshell:

ASSISTANT SENIOR PATROL LEADER

Job description: The assistant senior patrol leader is the second-highest-ranking junior leader in the troop. He is appointed by the senior patrol leader with the approval of the Scoutmaster. The assistant senior patrol leader acts as the senior patrol leader in the absence of the senior patrol leader or when called upon. He also provides leadership to other junior leaders in the troop.

Reports to: the senior patrol leader.

Assistant senior patrol leader duties:

❑ Helps the senior patrol leader lead meetings and activities

❑ Runs the troop in the absence of the senior patrol leader

❑ Helps train and supervise the troop scribe, quartermaster, instructor, librarian, historian, and chaplain aide

❑ Serves as a member of the patrol leaders' council

❑ Sets a good example

❑ Enthusiastically wears the Scout uniform correctly

❑ Lives by the Scout Oath and Law

❑ Shows Scout spirit

Chapter

The Patrol Leader's Job

When it was time for the Fox Patrol to get ready for its first camping trip, Bob had just been elected patrol leader. He'd been the assistant patrol leader in the spring.

The guys thought he had done a pretty good job. So when Tom, their old patrol leader, decided to run for senior patrol leader during the troop junior leader elections, Bob ran for patrol leader.

That night, the Foxes huddled in their patrol corner. They knew from past experience what they needed in a leader. He had to be someone with proven Scouting skills, someone who knew what the patrol could do. "I think Bob will be a great patrol leader," said one Scout. "He got Star at our last court of honor, so he can help the rest of us get our next rank, too."

"Yeah, and he even sat in on a couple of patrol leaders' council meetings last year when Tom couldn't make it. Bob knows how to speak up for our patrol."

After the vote, Bob hardly had time to catch his breath before he realized that the Foxes had to get ready for the first camping trip of the fall. It was going to be a real shakedown. He'd have to get his act together quickly if the Foxes were going to know what they were doing.

The first thing he did was appoint Tim as his assistant patrol leader. Besides being a good friend he knew he could depend on, Tim would finish his First Class requirements on this campout, the other guys liked him, and he would be good at filling in as patrol leader if that was needed later. Bob knew from his own experience that it would help Tim be ready when he got his chance to be patrol leader.

Does that sound a little familiar? It may not be exactly how you got to your junior leader position, but it's a good bet you found yourself in a similar position once you were "officially" a leader.

One Tough Job

You have an important job to do. All over the world, the patrol leader's job is known as the toughest in Scouting. It's where all the action takes place. It will take a real team effort to be a good patrol.

We all know what a group is. Most guys are part of many groups. Perhaps you're on a ball team at school or church. You might have a brother or sister who is in a debating club at school. Mom and Dad might belong to groups, too.

In Scouting, your troop is such a group. The patrol leaders' council is such a group. Many parents often serve on the troop committee, and that's a similar group. Your Scoutmaster and assistant Scoutmasters work together. So, you see, it really fits right in when we discuss your patrol as a group. After all, your patrol is one of the most natural groups we can think of. You and the rest of the guys in the patrol have many things in common. Of course, you're all Scouts. You all like to go camping and hiking. Everyone in your patrol is anxious to earn his next rank. You even have certain values in common, values that you pledge whenever you recite the Scout Oath and Scout Law.

Do you know what else your patrol has in common? You. Yes, you. You're the leader. So don't let the thought of being a leader get all out of whack. Because, you see, even the leader is part of the group.

As patrol leader of the Fox Patrol, Bob is part of several groups. The most obvious is his patrol. But, he's also part of the patrol leaders' council. Like every Scout, he's part of his troop. Every troop is part of a BSA local council, which is part of a movement called the Boy Scouts of America. We

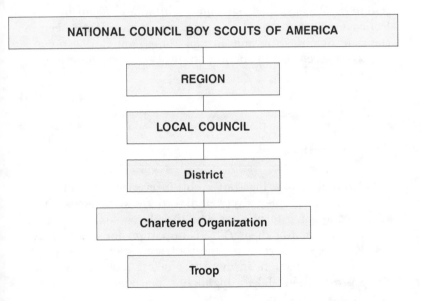

NATIONAL COUNCIL BOY SCOUTS OF AMERICA

REGION

LOCAL COUNCIL

District

Chartered Organization

Troop

call it a movement rather than an organization because, unlike a typical organization, the Boy Scouts of America is always changing to address the unique challenges of the day.

Now, this thing we call a movement is really nothing more than a group—a big group. As such, it can do big things. For more than eight decades, the Boy Scouts of America has been helping our country meet the many challenges it faces. The Boy Scouts of America has taken a leading role in efforts to promote literacy among all Americans. We've encouraged the wise conservation of our natural resources. We've helped fight hunger time and again by collecting food for the needy in our communities. We've been in the fight against drug and alcohol abuse. You can be proud that we've been one of the important leaders in addressing these issues.

Everyone Has a Job

No matter how big your group is, everyone has an important role to play. Everyone has to know the goals, the rules you're going to play by, who the players are, and what's expected of each of them. This is important for everyone, so it's even more important for the leaders to know these things.

With this thought in mind let's take a look at how your troop is organized. Take a highlighter pen and mark where you fit into this chart.

If you study this chart for a minute, you'll notice something pretty important. Everyone above you on the chart depends on you. And you can depend on everyone below you on the chart. Bob could feel all alone as the leader of the Fox Patrol if he didn't know where he fit in with the troop, couldn't he?

At that first patrol leaders' council meeting, he began to learn what his new role was all about. After the meeting, the senior patrol leader stopped for a minute to talk with Bob's mom when she arrived to pick up Bob.

TROOP JUNIOR LEADER ORGANIZATION

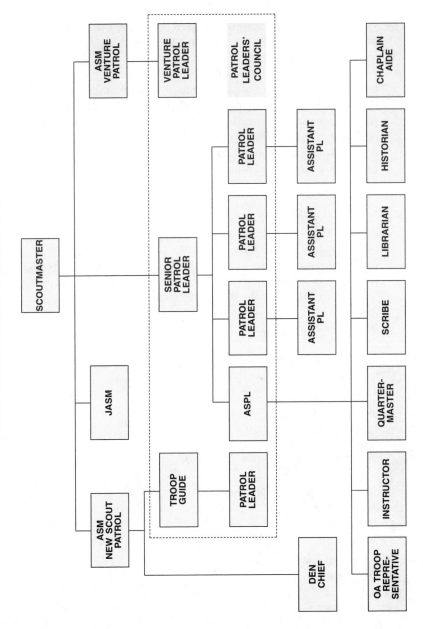

SCOUTMASTER

ASM VENTURE PATROL — VENTURE PATROL LEADER

PATROL LEADERS' COUNCIL

JASM

ASM NEW SCOUT PATROL

TROOP GUIDE — PATROL LEADER

SENIOR PATROL LEADER

ASPL

PATROL LEADER — ASSISTANT PL

PATROL LEADER — ASSISTANT PL

PATROL LEADER — ASSISTANT PL

DEN CHIEF

OA TROOP REPRE-SENTATIVE

INSTRUCTOR

QUARTER-MASTER

SCRIBE

LIBRARIAN

HISTORIAN

CHAPLAIN AIDE

"Hi, I'm Tom, the senior patrol leader. I'm sure glad to see Bob get elected patrol leader. He has a lot of responsibility in his new position," he said.

"He's already had some experience representing his patrol," said Tom with an obvious air of satisfaction. "Bob showed up for the patrol leaders' council meeting in complete uniform. He even had some questions based on what he knew the Foxes were interested in."

Bob cut in, "Come on, Mom. Let's go. I need to get home so I can get to work on a plan for our patrol meeting."

If You Think You Can, You Can

It sure looks like Bob got into his patrol leader role pretty quick. He already had a "can-do" attitude. He wasn't spending any time thinking about the things he might not be able to do, or those things he hadn't done before. From the very start, Bob was setting his sights on helping his patrol by getting started on the things he knew he could do.

If you approach being a patrol leader with a "can-do" attitude you'll be all right. Stop and think about it for a minute. A short while ago, you didn't know much about Scouts, did you? That didn't stop you from joining. You saw something you wanted to be part of and took a first step to ask about a meeting or talk to a friend about joining. Perhaps even without knowing it, you adopted the "can-do" attitude. You did what you knew how to do and decided to learn to do the new things you'd need to do. Keep that attitude, and you'll be well on your way to success as a patrol leader and in anything else you choose to do in life.

Being a Patrol Leader

Since you've gotten this far into the handbook, you already know a lot about the job of a patrol leader. You noticed how Bob got his job as the Fox patrol leader. It was probably the same way you got yours. He was elected by the Scouts in his patrol.

The election. Representative government is part of our everyday life in the United States. So much so, in fact, that we often take it for granted. But it comes with certain responsibilities, one of which is the responsibility to vote.

Voting is one important way that each individual gets to express his opinion where it really counts. Your mom and dad (also perhaps your older brother or sister) vote for local, state, and national leaders in much the same way the Scouts in Bob's patrol voted for him to be their patrol leader — by secret ballot. You'll want to use the secret ballot, too.

You may think that's too much work when only six or eight guys are going to be voting. But think about it for a minute. Doesn't it make the whole idea work better? A secret ballot assures each Scout that he can vote the way he wants to. He doesn't have to be afraid he'll hurt someone's feelings when it's learned he didn't vote the way he was expected to. There's no need to be concerned about what anyone will think about how he votes, because with a secret ballot no one needs to know.

Appointing an assistant patrol leader is one of the most important decisions a patrol leader makes.

The patrol leader's first job. Frequently the patrol leader will begin his term by appointing an assistant patrol leader. Often he makes the appointment the same night he's elected. That's okay. But you don't have to make a snap decision.

Appointing your assistant is one of the most important decisions you'll make as a patrol leader. It can wait until tomorrow or even next week. It is important that you appoint the right Scout.

Ask yourself some of the same questions you asked when you voted for patrol leader.

☐ Who's ready to be the assistant patrol leader? Look at the rank each Scout in your patrol has achieved. Rank isn't everything, but it can be a good indication of how dedicated a Scout is to Scouting. It is also an easy way to judge knowledge of basic Scouting skills.

☐ Who will the other patrol members respect? This is another way of asking who they will pay attention to. One good indication of what the other Scouts think is provided by the voting ballots from the patrol leader election. While they don't tell who voted for whom (because they're secret ballots and don't have the voter's names on them), they do tell who got the next highest total number of votes. It's a safe bet this Scout will be able to get the patrol's attention when you're not around.

A patrol leaders' council member. As a patrol leader, you're a voting member of your troop's patrol leaders' council. This is where you really get to represent the interests of your patrol.

Now, in order to represent your patrol, you have to know what those interests are. We'll get into this in more

As a patrol leader, you will represent the interests of the boys in your patrol.

detail in a later chapter when we discuss "The Patrol Leaders' Council Makes It Happen." But once you know what your patrol wants, you'll be in a great position to help the patrol leaders' council plan troop activities.

You'll also be able to use your meetings with other patrol leaders as an opportunity to brainstorm ideas for juicing up your patrol. If the old adage that two heads are better than one is true, just imagine what will happen when several patrol leaders join in trying to solve a problem or developing a new idea for your next patrol meeting.

Plan and steer patrol meetings. Every meeting should accomplish something. But if you go into a meeting without a plan, it will quickly become a shouting match or a great opportunity for a general roughhouse. You need to be prepared, and that means taking time to plan.

Quarterbacks don't go onto the football field without a plan. Business people don't go into meetings without plans. So why should a patrol leader think he can go into a patrol meeting without a plan? He shouldn't.

Remember, planning is the best chance you have to make sure your patrol meetings are both fun and productive. Keeping your patrol meetings fun is the best way to keep everyone interested in what the patrol meeting is all about. (See "Planning Is the Key," page 101.)

Help Scouts advance. One of the reasons you were elected is likely to be your skills as a Scout. Now you have the responsibility to pass these skills on to other Scouts. Sometimes you'll teach the skills yourself. At other times, you'll have someone else from the troop, your patrol, or even outside the troop come in to teach the skills your Scouts need.

A good patrol leader knows the advancement needs of each Scout in his patrol. This way, when he's helping to plan troop activities, he can encourage the patrol leaders' council to plan those that will help his patrol members advance.

Chief recruiter. As Scouts grow, get promoted, and move on in Scouting, you'll need some new guys to keep your patrol up to strength. Some will come out of the new Scout patrol. Others will be recruited by you and other Scouts in your patrol. You'll want to do some recruiting yourself, and you'll want to encourage your fellow patrol members to do some recruiting, too.

Look sharp; be sharp. This means set the example. Wear your uniform properly. Come to meetings prepared. Participate enthusiastically. Help other Scouts get the most out of each meeting or activity.

It means that you really try to live by the Scout Oath and Scout Law. You don't have to say anything about the fact that you're doing these things. Other Scouts will notice what you do and they'll follow your example.

Here's the job of the
in a nutshell:

PATROL LEADER

Job description: The patrol leader is the elected leader of his patrol. He represents his patrol on the patrol leaders' council.

Reports to: the senior patrol leader. If you're the patrol leader for the new Scout patrol, you'll also work with the troop guide who is assigned to your patrol.

Patrol leader duties:

❏ Appoints the assistant patrol leader

❏ Represents the patrol on the patrol leaders' council

❏ Plans and steers patrol meetings

❏ Helps Scouts advance

❏ Acts as the chief recruiter of new Scouts

❏ Keeps patrol members informed

❏ Knows what his patrol members and other leaders can do

❏ Sets the example

❏ Wears the uniform correctly

❏ Lives by the Scout Oath and Law

❏ Shows Scout spirit

Where Does the Assistant Patrol Leader Fit In?

The easy answer to this question is, right alongside the patrol leader. That's not really the wise-guy answer that it might first sound like. At the first meeting after Bob was elected, he had a Scoutmaster conference scheduled. This meant that Tim had to step in as patrol leader while Bob and the Scoutmaster were talking. In order to do this, Tim needed to know what was going on and what the patrol leader had planned.

A good assistant is always helping the leader. Where can you help better than at the leader's side? Also, a good assistant is always ready to back up the leader. This means he is ready to step into the leadership role when the leader isn't available.

If you ever want to be a patrol leader yourself, being an assistant patrol leader is a great way to get ready for the job.

Here's the job in a nutshell: ASSISTANT PATROL LEADER

Job description: The assistant patrol leader is appointed by the patrol leader and leads the patrol in his absence.

Reports to: the patrol leader.

Assistant patrol leader duties:

❏ Helps the patrol leader plan and steer patrol meetings and activities

❏ Helps him keep patrol members informed

❏ Helps the patrol get ready for all troop activities

❏ Represents his patrol at patrol leaders' council meetings when the patrol leader cannot attend

more . . .

- Lends a hand controlling the patrol and building patrol spirit
- Sets a good example
- Wears the uniform correctly
- Lives by the Scout Oath and Law
- Shows Scout spirit

Patrol Organization

Now that you have a good idea where you fit into the picture you might wonder where everyone else fits in. Two key words to remember concerning your patrol and your job as a patrol leader are "sharing leadership."

When Bob selected Tim as assistant patrol leader, he was taking the first step toward sharing leadership. We can all see how Bob will share leadership with his assistant. But Tim is not the only person who's going to be involved in patrol operations.

In every patrol, there are a number of jobs that can be assigned for weeks or months at a time. Let's look at some of them.

The **patrol scribe** must be someone who can do more than just write neatly. While good handwriting is important, you probably don't want to put it at the head of your list of qualifications for this job.

You're going to ask the scribe to keep the patrol log. This is a record of what goes on in each patrol meeting. You'll use it from meeting to meeting to recall what decisions were made at the last meeting, such as who agreed to bring

the refreshments, and who was going to call the local swimming pool to schedule a patrol swim.

When the scribe reads the log of the last patrol meeting, it gets everyone back on track and headed in the same direction.

The scribe also keeps attendance records and collects dues. He can prepare a budget for buying patrol equipment. When the patrol gets ready to go camping, he'll collect the money for buying food. The grubmaster will use the money to buy the food, then give the scribe a receipt for his records.

That word, **grubmaster,** is interesting isn't it? It's really sort of an old-fashioned word, but it seems to fit the job so well. Why would we want to use any other word? Let's try a few other words and see how they fit.

How about menu planner? Now that has about as much character as a wet paper towel doesn't it? Well, maybe we'll call this guy the food shopper. That sounds more like a chore than an opportunity.

Yes, grubmaster is the word, all right. This guy is going to take charge of seeing to it that the patrol eats right, so he deserves a name with a little character.

PATROL QUARTERMASTER

How about a **patrol quartermaster?** You probably already know who in your patrol is the most organized. He's the one who can always find his handbook quickly because he knows exactly where he put it. He'll be the first one to recall whether or not the troop has a bow saw the patrol can borrow for the next campout.

Why not take advantage of this guy's natural ability? He'll be a quartermaster who can keep all the patrol gear in order and make sure the patrol shines when it's time to check the troop gear back into the supply room. You know everything is going to be right where it's supposed to be.

Keeping morale high is the job of the **cheermaster.** He leads songs, yells, stunts, and campfire programs.

There are other jobs that can be assigned. Who do you want planning the details of your patrol hike or helping other Scouts plan a troop hike? You want someone who really has it down, don't you? The Scout with the most knowledge about hiking should plan your hike.

Sometimes these jobs only last for a short while, like one campout. There are other short-term jobs, too. Who will be responsible to see that there is enough firewood for cooking chores and that the fire is just the way the chief cook wants it for his job?

The **chief cook** gathers the food from the chow box and organizes cooking the meal. Sometimes, he'll do this alone. At other times he'll have one or more helpers. But, either way it's his job to make sure that the meal is prepared well and on time so that everyone can chow down together.

Naturally, you're going to need help with cleaning up. That is really an important job. Often more than one Scout will be doing this job, cleaning up the pots, pans, and patrol cooking utensils. Naturally, every Scout will take care of his own personal mess kit. See pages 281–83 of the *Boy Scout Handbook* for more details.

Sharing Leadership

That's a big part of what this business is all about. It gives everyone in your patrol a chance to feel that they too have an important role to play. Remember when you were just one of the guys in the patrol? How good did it feel to have the patrol leader look to you for some help?

It's important to recognize that no one can do everything by himself. Oh, you might be able to for a little while.

But even if everyone else involved is comfortable with this way of doing things, which is not likely, you'll soon find that it becomes overwhelming.

Leaders who try to do everything often end up not doing anything. They suffer what is called "burnout." They try so hard to do it all, to be everything to everybody, to remember every detail, that eventually they find they're not doing much of anything the way it should be done. This leads to a lack of enthusiasm about doing anything.

The patrol is the ideal place to gain a good understanding of how important it is to share leadership, because there are plenty of jobs to go around. Sharing leadership gives every Scout a chance to "buy in." You already know that if a plan is partly your creation, you're going to do your best to make sure everything comes out right, aren't you? Well, when you share leadership, you use other people's skills, ideas, and enthusiasm. That's how they buy in. You can bet they're going to work extra hard at making sure everything comes out right.

Plan a Campout Together

Take a look at how you can get everyone involved for a camping trip. First there's a plan for the trip. Sure, you could sit at home in your room and dream up a great trip all by yourself. But then it would be your trip, wouldn't it? If, on the other hand, you were to gather the patrol and work out a plan together, the camping trip would belong to everyone in the patrol.

This is another way of sharing leadership. It will give everyone a say in what kind of trip it's going to be. Perhaps equally important, it will let everyone feel like they're really part of the action. What they think and what they like really matter. You're still the leader; you're just sharing a little bit of that leadership.

The neat part is that the more you share your leadership, the more you're respected as a leader. When you come back from a successful trip, everyone's had a good time.

Plenty of advancement has taken place, and guess what! You're the patrol leader of a "great-time" patrol. Everyone will rally around their patrol leader to discover with him just what they're going to be doing next *and* how they're going to be part of it.

Someone is likely to volunteer to be grubmaster. He saw what the grubmaster did on the last trip, and now the new volunteer has some ideas of his own he'd like to try. It doesn't mean you don't have to be involved. Remember, you were elected partly because you have some experience and the skills that everyone thought would be helpful.

When the newest grubmaster starts out, he'll probably need a little assistance, perhaps with just getting everyone's attention or with breaking a tie vote on what to have for breakfast. There are a lot of little decisions you'll want him to make as you lead him in a new experience.

If you see that what he's doing is getting a little off track, you'll want to bring him back on track. Please do it gently, like a leader, not a dictator. Think how you'd react if you were on the receiving end of a comment like, "That won't work," or "What a dumb idea," or "Here, let me do it." It would make you feel pretty bad and possibly kill any desire you might have to continue.

Now, imagine your reaction if someone asks, "What do you think about . . ." or "Did you ever try . . ." or "Could I make a suggestion?" These kinds of questions are like an open door that welcomes new thoughts and allows the grubmaster to share your leadership. No one with any sense is going to say, "No, you can't make a suggestion."

Here are two more ideas for sharing leadership:

❑ Does one of the guys play the trumpet or maybe a guitar? Guitars are a great addition to a songfest around the campfire. You'd be surprised at how much better everyone sings with a little guitar accompaniment. The trumpet player would probably be flattered if you'd ask him to play "Taps" to close the campfire or to signal the end of the day.

❏ Who's the amateur photographer? A patrol shutterbug is a great addition to any patrol. He'll take pictures of the patrol in action.

Patrol Activities

One of the nice things about being the leader is that you can really start things happening. You don't have to wait for everyone else to get their act together. Patrol activities will add a special character to your patrol that no other patrol has. They allow you to do the things your Scouts are most interested in.

With well-planned patrol activities, the guys will advance faster and everyone will have more fun. A special patrol spirit will develop. You'll want to consider hikes, weekend camping trips, service projects, and simple Good Turns. Use your *Boy Scout Handbook, Fieldbook,* and *Troop Program Resources* for ideas. Check out "Planning Is the Key," page 101.

Patrol Meetings

Patrol meetings happen just about anywhere, it seems. Regular patrol meetings are held at troop meetings, but some are called on the spur of the moment when a patrol is suddenly faced with a new and unexpected challenge; for example, when the senior patrol leader asks for help building the fire for the Saturday night campfire.

Why patrol meetings? You've already discovered some of the reasons: working on advancement, planning activities, and discussing menus for campouts. How about using the meetings to practice for a troop competition, rehearse a skit for the campfire, design a patrol flag, earn money to buy patrol equipment, or brainstorm ideas to present to the patrol leaders' council. The list can go on. If you have ideas now, write them in here while you're thinking about it.

Ideas for Patrol Meetings

_____

_____

_____

_____

_____

_____

_____

_____

_____

_____

Patrol Meeting Agenda

It's likely that every patrol meeting will be a little different. Still, having a somewhat standard agenda makes planning easier and allows everyone to have some idea what to expect. If you make copies of the agenda for everyone, that's even better. In this way, everyone can get ready for his part in the meeting.

Every meeting should have certain things. You'll want a little ceremony and enough time for skill development, a game, and taking care of business.

Try this agenda. If making changes will make it work better for your patrol, go right ahead.

Sample Patrol Meeting Agenda

Opening—Hold a brief ceremony. _____

_____

Business—Scribe reads the log of the last meeting. Scouts report on old business. Any new business is introduced for discussion and decisions. This is also a good time to inspect uniforms, collect patrol dues, review advancement requirements, and vote on items needing everyone's input.

_____

Skill activity—Demonstration and/or practice of a Scouting skill. Perhaps the patrol will spend some time building a camp gadget, designing a patrol flag, or practicing for a competition.

_____

_____

Game—You'll want this to be a Scouting game. You can play ball any time. For some ideas on games, check out *Troop Program Resources*. It's also likely your senior patrol leader and the adult leaders in your troop will have some suggestions you'll enjoy.

_____

_____

Closing—This is a quiet moment and a good time for Scouts to practice ceremonies for use at a troop meeting. You'll want to keep it short and dignified.

_____

_____

National Honor Patrol

If you really want evidence that the patrol you lead is a great patrol, then you'll want to "go the extra mile" and earn the National Honor Patrol Award (formerly the Baden-Powell Patrol Award). This award is given to patrols whose members make an extra effort to have the best patrol possible.

The award is an embroidered star worn beneath your patrol medallion, and it spotlights your patrol as one of the best. It's a challenge the guys can really get behind.

A patrol can earn the award by doing the following over a period of three months:

1. Have a patrol name, flag, and yell. Put the patrol design on equipment and use the patrol yell. Keep patrol records up-to-date.

2. Hold two patrol meetings every month.

3. Take part in at least one hike, outdoor activity, or other Scouting event.

4. Complete two Good Turns or service projects approved by the patrol leaders' council.

5. Help two patrol members advance one rank.

6. Wear the full uniform correctly at troop activities (at least 75 percent of the patrol's membership).

7. Have a representative attend at least three patrol leaders' council meetings.

8. Have eight members in the patrol or experience an increase in patrol membership.

Chapter

The Troop Guide Helps Make First Impressions

It's interesting that one of the newest junior leader positions, the troop guide, is also one of the most important. The troop guide is especially important because he's responsible for a new Scout's first experiences. First experiences are a lot like first impressions. In fact, they are first impressions. A bad first impression can turn us off. At best, it will take a lot of effort to get us turned back on again.

That's the way it is when a boy shows up for his first few troop meetings. He's probably heard from another Scout about the fun he has at troop meetings. By the time his first meeting is over, he has seen his first *Boy Scout Handbook*, and he's been introduced to the fun he should expect.

Then someone, maybe an older Scout who's used to kidding around with some of the older guys, laughs when the new Scout makes a mistake. That can really hurt.

Next, when the senior patrol leader calls the troop to attention, and one of the patrol leaders begins to lead the troop in reciting the Scout Oath, the new boy is in trouble again. The patrol leader began by saying "Scout sign." The puzzled look on the new guy's face told everyone he didn't

The troop guide helps new Scouts get comfortable with outdoor skills.

know what that meant. They didn't mean to laugh at him, but they did and it hurt.

As if that's not enough, during the meeting there was a contest. Each patrol was building an "A-frame chariot" using spars and lashings. The excitement was high. The new guy wanted to join in. But he didn't know how. It was a race. He was pushed aside by one of the older Scouts. For the rest of the meeting, he just sat and watched. It wasn't much fun.

It's a pretty sad picture, isn't it? It might be a first impression that could make this the last Scout meeting for this guy. There are plenty of things he can do that are more fun than being laughed at or mocked because he's new and treading on unfamiliar turf.

New Scout Patrol

Nobody wants this to be the experience of a new Scout. That's why we have a new Scout patrol. This patrol is made up only of new boys joining the troop. Most are not yet 12 years old and have not entered the seventh grade.

This is where the troop guide comes in. He's an older Scout. He knows the ropes. He understands what it's like to be new in the troop. It's his job to work with the new Scout patrol, helping each Scout learn how a troop operates. He's there to explain the difference between what you do when you hear someone say "Scout sign" and when you hear someone say "Sign's up."

"Big Brother"

The troop guide will be at least a First Class Scout. The Scoutmaster, with the advice of the assistant Scoutmaster for the new Scout patrol, appoints a junior leader who is mature enough to work with the new Scouts. The Scoutmaster expects the troop guide to be their friend or "big brother." Right away, as troop guide, you'll set out to make certain the older Scouts remember what it was like to be the new guy. You'll want them to help you make the new Scouts feel welcome and part of the Scouting family. This means no teasing or intimidation.

For the first few meetings, you'll help new Scouts understand things that everyone else takes for granted. Following directions given by silent hand signals isn't hard, once you know what the signals mean. But until someone like a friend or a "big brother" clues you in on what they mean, you might just as well be in the dark.

But there's much more than hand signals to learn, isn't there? Let's look in on a new Scout patrol just being formed and see how the "big brother" troop guide works.

"Greg, your older brother, Justin, is in the Fox Patrol, isn't he?" asked Paul, the troop guide. "Did he have anything to do with your joining the troop?"

"I really joined because Keith asked me to," Greg said with an embarrassed chuckle. "But Justin always comes home with these stories about how much fun the hike was, or with a new patch, or another merit badge. So, yeah, I guess he made it look pretty good."

The other boys in the new Scout patrol started to talk about their reasons for joining. Paul raised his right hand high above his head in the Scout sign. Quietly he said just two words, "Sign's up."

No one paid much attention. The rest of the Scout hall was alive with patrols getting ready for their parts in the night's meeting. Greg's comments spurred some interesting thoughts that everyone wanted to share.

This time Paul spoke considerably louder. "Rule number one, when the sign goes up the mouth goes shut. Sign's up!" His right hand shot up into the air. Each Scout's right hand did the same. And the patrol fell silent. All eyes were on Paul.

"See how easy it is? You're going to see the Scoutmasters, senior patrol leader, and patrol leaders using the Scout sign this way whenever they need your attention. As soon as you see it, stop what you are doing, put the sign up, and stop talking immediately. It only takes a few seconds for the whole troop to become quiet this way."

The new Scout patrol remained quiet as they waited to see what was next.

Paul continued, "Okay guys, you're a patrol. As a patrol, you need a patrol leader. So, we're going to hold an election. In Scouting, we elect our patrol leaders and the senior patrol leader."

The election took only a couple minutes after Paul explained what the patrol leader's job would be and that they'd have another election every month or two so that everyone would get a chance to be patrol leader.

"Now that we have a patrol leader, let me explain some of the things we do as a troop," he went on. He then turned to the new patrol leader. "The first few minutes of every meeting are spent getting our act together. Patrols that have skill demonstrations gather the equipment they need and begin to get set up. Some patrols use the time to collect their dues and conduct a quick uniform inspection before the opening ceremony."

Paul briefly explained several routine things. He was lending his experience to the new Scouts so that they could adjust quickly to the standard troop operations. During the weeks and months to come, he'd do this type of thing many times. Of course it wouldn't always be this basic. As the new Scouts gained in experience, their needs would change.

The Challenge

The big challenge for any troop guide is helping each Scout in the new Scout patrol get to First Class rank within his first year in the troop.

You'll work with the assistant Scoutmaster for new Scouts (one is always assigned to work with the new Scout patrol and the troop guide) and other junior leaders to help the Scouts learn the skills for Tenderfoot, Second Class, and First Class ranks. Some Scouts need more encouragement than others, but each can earn First Class during his first year.

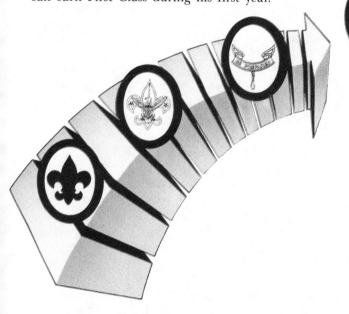

You'll meet monthly with the assistant Scoutmaster to plan activities that will be fun and that will allow each Scout to meet the requirements for advancement. Often Scouts won't even know they are working on advancement because the activities you help plan are so much fun.

Should a new Scout get discouraged, you'll provide some special encouragement. You'll want to show him that he *can* do it. It will be great fun. Perhaps, together with the assistant Scoutmaster, you'll design a special challenge to get him going (maybe get him caught up) before the meeting is over. This way he leaves with a feeling of accomplishment. He'll want to come back.

From the Square Knot to CPR

The new Scouts will complete the requirements they need to get to First Class rank just by actively participating in troop activities. Still, there are times that one-on-one "teaching" will be needed. When it is, the troop guide has to be a "jack of all trades."

Does this mean you have to be expert in everything? It sure would be a good idea, although impractical. Remember, though, that you have resources. You can call in other Scouts to help. You can ask the assistant Scoutmaster for help. You can even bring in someone from outside the troop if that's necessary, though it rarely is.

Most often, you'll have the skill yourself. After all, it wasn't that long ago that you completed the same requirements. If you're rusty and really don't have time to brush up on the skill, ask someone whose skills are sharp to step in for you.

First Class Tracking

The requirements for Tenderfoot, Second Class, and First Class ranks can all be worked on at the same time. Though it seldom happens, a new Scout could receive more than one rank advancement at a court of honor.

FIRST CLASS—FIRST YEAR TRACKING SHEET

Date _____

Name _____ Date joined_____ Class goal _____

(Date)

Category	Goal Attainment*			Requirements		Date Scheduled	Date Completed
	Trp	Out	Own	Rank	Number		
Outdoor							
	x	x		T	1		
		x		T	2		
		x		T	3		
	x	x		T	4a		
	x	x		T	4b		
	x	x		T	5		
	x	x		T	11		
		x		S	1a		
		x		S	1b		
		x		S	2a		
		x		S	2b		
		x		S	2c		
		x		S	2d		
	x	x		S	2e		
		x		S	2f		
		x		S	2g		
	x	x		S	5		
	x	x		F	1		
		x		F	2		
		x		F	3		
	x	x		F	4a		
	x	x		F	4b		
	x	x		F	4c		
	x	x		F	4d		
		x		F	4e		
	x	x		F	6		
	x	x		F	7a		
	x	x		F	7b		
	x	x		F	7c		
Physical fitness							
	x	x	x	T	10a		
	x	x	x	T	10b		
	x	x		S	7a		
	x	x		S	7b		
	x	x		S	7c		
	x	x		S	8		
	x	x		F	9a		
	x	x		F	9b		
	x	x		F	9c		
	x	x		F	9d		
Citizenship							
	x	x		T	6		
	x	x		T	12a		
	x	x		T	12b		
	x	x	x	S	3		
	x	x	x	S	4		
	x	x		S	6a		
	x	x		S	6b		
	x	x		S	6c		
	x	x	x	F	5		
	x	x		F	8a		
	x	x		F	8b		
	x	x		F	8c		
	x	x		F	8d		
Patrol/troop participation							
	x			T	8		
	x			S	9		
	x			F	10		
Personal development							
	x	x		T	7		
	x		x	T	9		
			x	T	13		
			x	S	10		
			x	F	11		
Completed							
				Tenderfoot			
				Second Class			
				First Class			

*Goal attainment—locations where Scout may work on his rank requirements:
Trp—Troop meetings
Out—Outings
Own—On his own

Because each rank can be worked on at the same time, it's necessary to keep close track of those requirements that have been completed. The assistant Scoutmaster for the new Scout patrol will keep the advancement records straight. You'll want to be familiar with how each Scout is doing, so you'll frequently want to review the First Class–First Year Tracking Sheet, a goal-oriented method for keeping track of advancement.

The tracking sheet is easy to use. All the requirements to First Class rank fall into one of five main categories, which follow:

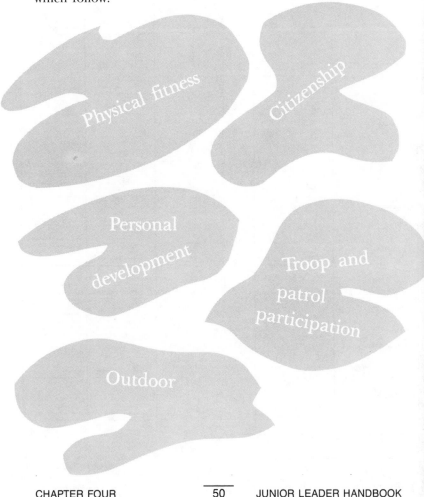

Physical fitness

Citizenship

Personal development

Troop and patrol participation

Outdoor

Take a quick look at the tracking sheet, and you'll see each of these categories. Next to each, you see one, two, or three "X's." These tell you whether it's best for the Scout to complete the requirement at a troop meeting, during a troop outing, or on his own. The next column shows which rank the skill will be credited toward. The final column tells you the number of the exact requirement. They're in the *Boy Scout Handbook*.

For example, the very first requirement listed is in the "Outdoor" category. The X's indicate it can be completed at a troop meeting or during a troop outing. The last two columns tell you it is requirement No. 1 for the Tenderfoot rank.

Following all these columns are blanks for the date the Scout plans to complete each requirement (Date Scheduled) and the date he actually completes it (Date Completed).

Learning to Be a Leader

As troop guide, you want to do a good job. But you might not have learned all the leadership skills a good leader needs. With a little practice, under the guidance of your assistant Scoutmaster, you'll begin to see that you're learning to lead. You'll want to take advantage of the leadership training activities discussed in chapter 1.

Take a minute right now to take an inventory of your leadership skills. Look at the following list. Do you know all these skills? Are you using them regularly? If the answers are yes, that's great. If you need help in any area, now is the time to check with your coach, the assistant Scoutmaster, and brush up on those skills you may be a little weak in.

❑ **Know how to get and give information.** You'll want to pass this skill along to each new patrol leader in the new Scout patrol. How are you going to remember what you were told by the assistant Scoutmaster? How is the patrol leader to remember what his patrol suggests before he attends the patrol leaders' council meeting? If you keep a small notebook and pencil handy, you don't have to rely on your memory. The patrol leader of the new Scout patrol will likely follow your example.

❑ **Know how to counsel a patrol leader on how to represent his patrol at the patrol leaders' council meeting.** If you've been a patrol leader yourself, you have a jump on troop guides who haven't. If not, your assistant Scoutmaster will work with you. You might want to keep a couple of things in mind, though. Remember how you like to be treated by the assistant Scoutmaster? Or, perhaps it's a little more to the point to remember how you were treated by the senior patrol leader when you were a new patrol leader.

No one likes to be bossed around. You'll find that questions and suggestions are more readily accepted than blunt criticism. When the new patrol leader goes to his first patrol leaders' council meeting, he'll be uncomfortable enough. Going without being prepared will only make it worse. Suggest that he take a few minutes to get suggestions from the guys in the patrol.

Suggest some questions he might ask to get them talking. In the beginning, some of the questions might be:

"Are there any particular games you've heard of Scouts playing that you'd like to have us play during a troop meeting?"

"What would you think of our patrol leading the opening ceremony at a troop meeting?"

"Does anyone have a particular requirement they need to complete for advancement?"

As troop guide, you'll want to be careful about how you counsel the new patrol leader. Talk to him about the patrol leaders' council meetings that you've attended. Explain what goes on. Tell him about the time you came prepared with an idea from one of the Scouts in your patrol and how it became part of the very next meeting.

Make sure he knows that you'll be with him to help him make decisions that are best for his patrol. You might even want to suggest that you'll have your mom or dad swing by and pick him up on your way to the patrol leaders' council meeting. He'll be a lot more comfortable knowing that he doesn't have to walk into his first meeting all alone.

☐ **Know how to teach.** This doesn't mean you have to grab a piece of chalk and head to the chalkboard. No sir, not for a patrol meeting. Most "teaching" is done as part of planned activities or games. You'll need to be familiar with the basic skills, which you are, of course, because you learned them in order to earn your First Class rank. You'll want to practice your demonstrations. Remember that people learn better and faster if they can actually do the skill. When you're teaching the basics such as the Scout handclasp, Scout salute, or Scout sign, explain what you're going to do, demonstrate it with one of the Scouts, and then let the Scouts practice among themselves.

This method works for virtually everything. Knife and ax skills are another good example. A new Scout will never learn how to sharpen his Scout knife just by watching you sharpen yours. You have to put a blade to a whetstone for a while to really understand what it takes to get your knife as sharp as it should be.

☐ **Know how to plan.** Planning is one of those tasks that most of us have to work at in order to get it right. You'll learn more about this during junior leader training, and we'll discuss it in greater detail in chapter 9. For right now, let's take a quick look at the steps involved.

STEP 1

Know what you want to do. Are you planning a patrol meeting or simply a game for the next troop meeting?

STEP 2

Know what equipment you're going to need. It will be quite different for a weekend hike than it will be for teaching a Tenderfoot first aid requirement.

STEP 3

Consider several ways you can accomplish your goal. For example, you might teach first aid with a demonstration or you might choose to use a game. Then, too, you could ask another patrol to put on a skit that demonstrates a first aid skill. Then have the new Scouts practice the skill on each other.

STEP 4

Take some action to get it going. If you think it's best to have another patrol demonstrate the first aid skill in a skit, you'll have to meet with the other patrol leader and explain what you would like his patrol to do.

☐ **Know how to control the patrol.** Simply put, you need to be sure everyone in the patrol understands what's expected. Then be certain they know that you're going to pay attention to how well they do it. You may want them to learn how to prepare wood for a cooking fire. They need to know exactly what you want them to do, and they need to know that you are going to be checking to see that it's done correctly. Let them know what you *expect* and that you're going to *inspect*.

Training Patrol Leaders of the New Scout Patrol

During the year, you're going to get to work with several members of the new Scout patrol as they are elected patrol leader. It will get a little easier each time because each new patrol leader will come to his new role with a little more understanding of what the patrol leader's job is. He will have seen his peers perform in the job. Add to this the example you have been setting, and his knowledge level has jumped up the ladder a couple of rungs.

Now all you have to do is bring him up to speed on some of the specific skills of a patrol leader. Your counseling and training of each new patrol leader will probably continue throughout the time they serve as patrol leaders.

This could get a little sticky. You need to remember which patrol leader you counseled, and on what subject. Keep in mind that you want the patrol members to view their *patrol leader* as the leader, not you.

With this in mind, you will never "teach" patrol leader skills in front of the other Scouts. Doing this can make it look like you're the patrol leader and it will "deep-six" any chance the real patrol leader has of actually leading his patrol.

After the patrol meeting or troop meeting, take a few minutes with the patrol leader to go over the plan for the next meeting or activity. This will help him get prepared. Suggest that he read chapters 1 and 9 in this handbook. They will give him a basic understanding of what's expected. Later, when you're meeting with him, review what he read and answer his questions.

The troop guide's job is completed when a Scout reaches First Class.

Here's the job of the in a nutshell:

TROOP GUIDE

Job description: The troop guide works with new Scouts. He helps them feel comfortable and earn their First Class rank in their first year.

Reports to: the assistant Scoutmaster for the new Scout patrol in the troop.

Troop guide duties:

- ☐ Introduces new Scouts to troop operations
- ☐ Guides new Scouts through early Scouting activities
- ☐ Shields new Scouts from harassment by older Scouts
- ☐ Helps new Scouts earn First Class rank in their first year
- ☐ Teaches basic Scout skills
- ☐ Coaches the patrol leader of the new Scout patrol on his duties
- ☐ Works with the patrol leader at patrol leaders' council meetings
- ☐ Attends patrol leaders' council meetings with the patrol leader of the new Scout patrol
- ☐ Assists the assistant Scoutmaster with training
- ☐ Counsels individual Scouts on Scouting challenges
- ☐ Sets a good example
- ☐ Enthusiastically wears the Scout uniform correctly
- ☐ Lives by the Scout Oath and Law
- ☐ Shows Scout spirit

OLD
SCOUT
STUFF

Chapter

Behind the Scenes

Support Jobs

Many of the junior leadership positions in Scouting aren't as visible as those we have discussed so far. Boys holding these positions wear their position badges on their sleeve just like the senior patrol leader, patrol leaders, and troop guide. But their work normally isn't as much "up front." They are behind the scenes performing important jobs such as keeping records or maintaining the troop's equipment. Every junior leader should know who these leaders are and what their responsibilities are.

This chapter will briefly review the duties of these junior leaders: junior assistant Scoutmaster, Order of the Arrow troop representative, troop scribe, troop quartermaster, instructor, chaplain aide, and librarian/historian.

TROOP QUARTERMASTER

Job description: The quartermaster keeps track of troop equipment and sees that it is in good working order.

Reports to: the assistant senior patrol leader.

Quartermaster duties:

- ❑ Keeps records on patrol and troop equipment
- ❑ Makes sure equipment is in good working condition
- ❑ Issues equipment and makes sure it's returned in good condition
- ❑ Makes suggestions for new or replacement items
- ❑ Works with the troop committee member responsible for equipment
- ❑ Sets a good example
- ❑ Enthusiastically wears the Scout uniform correctly
- ❑ Lives by the Scout Oath and Law
- ❑ Shows Scout spirit

JUNIOR ASSISTANT SCOUTMASTER

Job description: The junior assistant Scoutmaster serves in the capacity of an assistant Scoutmaster except where legal age and maturity are required. He must be at least 16 years old and not yet 18. He's appointed by the Scoutmaster because of his leadership ability.

Reports to: the Scoutmaster.

Junior assistant Scoutmaster duties:

- ❑ Functions as an assistant Scoutmaster
- ❑ Performs duties as assigned by the Scoutmaster
- ❑ Sets a good example
- ❑ Enthusiastically wears the Scout uniform correctly
- ❑ Lives by the Scout Oath and Law
- ❑ Shows Scout spirit

CHAPLAIN AIDE

Job description: The chaplain aide works with the troop chaplain to meet the religious needs of Scouts in the troop. He also works to promote the religious emblems program.

Reports to: the assistant senior patrol leader.

Chaplain aide duties:

- ☐ Assists the troop chaplain with religious services at troop activities
- ☐ Tells Scouts about the religious emblem program for their faith
- ☐ Makes sure religious holidays are considered during troop program planning
- ☐ Helps plan for religious observance in troop activities
- ☐ Sets a good example
- ☐ Enthusiastically wears the Scout uniform correctly
- ☐ Lives by the Scout Oath and Law
- ☐ Shows Scout spirit

TROOP SCRIBE

Job description: The scribe keeps the troop records. He records the activities of the patrol leaders' council and keeps a record of dues, advancement, and Scout attendance at troop meetings.

Reports to: the assistant senior patrol leader.

Scribe duties:

- ☐ Attends and keeps a log of patrol leaders' council meetings
- ☐ Records individual Scout attendance and dues payments more . . .
- ☐ Records individual Scout advancement progress
- ☐ Works with the troop committee member responsible for records and finance
- ☐ Sets a good example
- ☐ Enthusiastically wears the Scout uniform correctly
- ☐ Lives by the Scout Oath and Law
- ☐ Shows Scout spirit

INSTRUCTOR

Job description: The instructor teaches Scouting skills.

Reports to: the assistant senior patrol leader.

Instructor duties:

☐ Teaches basic Scouting skills in troop and patrols

☐ Sets a good example

☐ Enthusiastically wears the Scout uniform correctly

☐ Lives by the Scout Oath and Law

☐ Shows Scout spirit

ORDER OF THE ARROW TROOP REPRESENTATIVE

Job description: The Order of the Arrow troop representative enhances the image of the Order by serving as a youth liaison between the troop and the local OA lodge or chapter.

Reports to: the assistant senior patrol leader.

Order of the Arrow troop representative duties:

☐ Serves as a communication link between the lodge or chapter and the troop

☐ Encourages year-round and resident camping in the troop

☐ Encourages older-Scout participation in high-adventure programs

☐ Encourages Scouts to actively participate in community service projects

☐ Assists with leadership skills training in the troop

☐ Encourages Arrowmen to assume leadership positions in the troop

☐ Encourages Arrowmen in the troop to be active participants in lodge and/or chapter activities and to seal their membership in the Order by becoming Brotherhood members

☐ Sets a good example

- ☐ Wears the Scout uniform correctly
- ☐ Lives by the Scout Oath, Scout Law, and OA Obligation
- ☐ Shows and helps develop Scout spirit

LIBRARIAN/HISTORIAN

Job description: The librarian/historian takes care of troop literature and keeps a historical record or scrapbook of troop activities.

Reports to: the assistant senior patrol leader.

Librarian duties:

- ☐ Sets up and takes care of a troop library
  - —Keeps records of books and pamphlets owned by the troop
  - —Adds new or replacement items as needed
  - —Keeps books and pamphlets available for borrowing
  - —Keeps a system for checking books and pamphlets in and out
  - —Follows up on late returns
- ☐ Sets a good example
- ☐ Enthusiastically wears the Scout uniform correctly
- ☐ Lives by the Scout Oath and Law
- ☐ Shows Scout spirit

Historian duties:

- ☐ Gathers pictures and facts about past troop activities and keeps them in a historical file or scrapbook
- ☐ Takes care of troop trophies, ribbons, and souvenirs of troop activities
- ☐ Keeps information about former members of the troop
- ☐ Sets a good example
- ☐ Enthusiastically wears the Scout uniform correctly
- ☐ Lives by the Scout Oath and Law
- ☐ Shows Scout spirit

Chapter

The Den Chief Pledge

I promise to help the Cub Scouts (or Webelos Scouts) in my den to the best of my ability; to encourage, guide, and protect them in all den and pack activities; and to show them by my example what a Boy Scout is.

I will strive to be prompt and dependable, and to cooperate with the leaders in carrying out the den program.

As each Cub Scout completes the third grade, I will encourage him to join a Webelos den.

As he becomes eligible, I will do all in my power to interest him in becoming a Boy Scout.

The Den Chief Helps Cultivate Boy Scouts

Where do Boy Scouts come from? If we do the right things, many of them come from the Cub Scouts. As a den chief, you can make a big difference in how many Cub Scouts actually become Boy Scouts.

As a den chief, you're a special kind of junior leader because you're both an active member of your patrol and troop and you fill an important role in the Cub Scout pack. One of those roles is in acting and looking like a Boy Scout. Your example will go a long way toward inviting the Cub Scouts into Boy Scouting when they're old enough. Every time you do your job as a den chief, you're doing a good turn for younger boys who will look up to you and want to be like you.

Leading as a Den Chief

The leader is the guy others look to, to get things done. As den chief, you have other leaders depending on you, too. The adult den leader, the Cubmaster, your Scoutmaster, and your senior patrol leader are all expecting big things. Perhaps even more important than their expectations, though, are the expectations of the Cub Scouts you'll be working with.

Your Scoutmaster and senior patrol leader have faith in you. That's why they selected you to be a den chief. You have the special leadership qualities that will allow you to succeed as a leader with these younger Scouts.

You don't need to worry. You wouldn't have been selected for this junior leader position if everyone didn't agree that you can do it. You'll want to set a good example for the younger boys. Remember, to them you *are* the Boy Scouts. You're the big guy. You're the leader they want to look up to and will look up to.

Occasionally you'll find that you don't know the answer to a question, or the solution to a problem. At that point, you simply do what any good leader does. You use your

The *Den Chief Handbook* is one of the den chief's most important resources.

resources. You find someone who knows the answer. This may be the den leader, the assistant Scoutmaster for the new Scout patrol, or the senior patrol leader. Maybe the answer is in your *Den Chief Handbook*. Whatever the question may be, the answer won't be difficult to find.

Learning as a Den Chief

One of the nice things about being a den chief is the chance to learn about leading. You'll have the chance to try some of your ideas, to plan, and to make those plans happen.

The skills of leadership aren't different for a den chief. So you'll want to attend junior leader training with the other junior leaders in the troop. You'll probably have an opportunity to attend a special den chief training conference. Be sure to attend. Also, be sure to read the chapters in this handbook on planning and leadership skills.

Training makes you more effective as a leader. You'll find your job is easier because you have the know-how. As you experience leadership in your role as den chief, you'll easily see ways to use these newly developed skills in your patrol and troop.

You're the Activities Assistant

One of the most enjoyable parts of being a den chief is the opportunity to help lead activities. Your den leader will look to you frequently when it's activity time.

What kind of activities, you ask? Well, how about leading songs. That's definitely not foreign to you. If you haven't led songs yourself at troop campfires, you've seen others lead them. The same thing is true for stunts or skits. You may also be asked to lead games and sports activities.

Leading songs. This can be a lot of fun, with the right attitude. You don't have to be a great singer to lead songs. All you really need is some enthusiasm. Get up on your feet. Gather the Cub Scouts around you. You can see by the expressions on their faces that they're ready for you to do a great job. They expect it. And you know what? You can't lose. They don't know how a song is supposed to be led. So even if you make a little mistake, they won't know it.

Keep the first songs simple. Make sure you know the words and the tune before you start. Have everyone repeat the words after you say them, *not sing them*, one time. This way everyone will know the words. Then sing, or maybe hum, one verse so that they hear what it sounds like. Now it's time for everyone to sing. Don't worry what you sound like. The Cub Scouts are going to be too busy listening to the words coming out of their mouths to be concerned about what the words sound like coming out of yours.

Then, raise your hands high above your head and have everyone sing. When you're all done, give them a hand. Tell them what a great job they did. They'll want to do it again.

Leading stunts and skits. Most of us find this a little easier than leading songs. Here are some hints.

Keep it simple. Make sure the script is written out so every-

one knows what they're going to say. If you need a narrator, select him beforehand so he can read through his part in advance. Assign a part in the stunt or skit to each Cub Scout.

Be patient. Remember how you felt the first time you had to get up in front of your friends and take part in a skit. Help each Cub Scout with his part.

Normally you'll rehearse the parts during several den meetings and perform the skit at a pack meeting. You may also get to help make costumes or props. But don't depend on your ideas alone. Ask each Cub Scout to come up with his own ideas. Then congratulate them on the idea. Praise from the den chief is something they'll feel good about for a long time. You can bet that as soon as they get home from a meeting, they'll tell someone that you said they did a good job or had a great idea.

Leading games. The games should have a lot of action if the place where they are being played will allow it. Obviously you can't play kickball in the den leader's living room. Your *Den Chief Handbook* will have ideas for games. You'll want to explain the rules and then act as the judge or referee to make sure the game is played fairly. If you're selecting the game, try to use games that help the Cub Scouts with their advancement. If you have someone in the den who is disabled, make sure to play games he can play, too.

Leading sports. Most young boys like sports, and you know a lot more about sports than the Cub Scouts in your den. So, you're going to be asked to lead sports activities. You'll want to make sure you know the rules before you start. Then make sure the Cub Scouts know the rules.

Sports may include things like stickball, soccer, and relay games. It may also include physical fitness exercises such as pushups or situps.

Be a Friend

You already know what it means to be a friend. You have friends in your troop and patrol. You probably have more friends at school, in church, or around the neighborhood. But being friends with a Cub Scout is special.

First of all, the Cub Scout is really going to be proud to have you, a Boy Scout, as a friend. There are some things, however, that you're going to have to keep in mind. You'll need to do some things differently to get along with boys of Cub Scout age. Here are some tips:

- ❏ Young boys don't like to be made fun of or made to look silly.

- ❏ They worry about what people think of them, especially people they like.

- ❏ They need to know that you mean what you say. They'll probably test you to make sure.

- ❏ They are big on rules. If they know and understand what the rules are, they'll try to obey them.

- ❏ When they misbehave, they know it. And they expect you to say something. When you don't say anything, it may be taken to mean that it's okay to do it again.

- ❏ They want to try things for themselves—to be independent.

- ❏ They want to belong to a group. The boys in the den will naturally become friends.

- ❏ They don't all have the same reading skills. You'll need to help some of them. It's important that you are careful not to embarrass the less experienced readers.

- ❏ While some boys will talk with you quite easily, others will not express themselves very well. Please be patient.

- ❏ They are especially happy when they can do active, physical things such as running, jumping, and climbing.

- ❏ You'll need to think of ways for them to use all their energy.

- ❏ If you ask them to keep themselves neat and clean, they'll try.

- ❏ They thrive on praise. Go out of your way to make them feel good about the things they have done.

❏ You should expect them to get done those things that you ask them to do.

❏ They love to compete with each other, but if they lose, their feelings may be hurt. This would be a good time to comfort and encourage them.

❏ Young boys love to talk about things they have done. As their friend, they'll want you to listen.

❏ At this age, they are just beginning to be interested in hobbies and collections.

❏ They are close to their parents and care a lot about what their family thinks of them.

❏ They like to do things with their parents and families.

Your Role in Den and Pack Meetings

It doesn't matter to you where the den meets. Your job remains the same. Really, there are several parts to your job, because there are several parts to the meeting.

You help the den leader as you are asked. First, plan to arrive early in full uniform, or get into full uniform as soon as you arrive. Before the meeting starts, there will be several things you can do to help. The meeting room has to be set up, equipment and supplies have to be ready for use, and duties for the meeting explained.

Your leadership will also be needed as the Cub Scouts arrive, during the opening ceremony, taking care of business (collecting dues, etc.), assisting with activities, during the closing, and after the meeting. Your *Den Chief Handbook* will explain these things in greater detail.

At the pack meeting, normally held once a month, all the dens get together to strut their stuff. Your den may have been working on a skit at each den meeting. Now it's the big time. All the moms and dads are there, as well as all the other Cub Scouts. You'll be proud of how well all your work turns out.

Much like the den meeting, you'll want to arrive early so you can help out. The den leaders or the Cubmaster will let you know what needs to be done. This is a good time to let everyone know just what a Boy Scout can do. Of course, you'll still want to keep an eye on "your boys."

The Webelos Den

The Webelos Scouts are still part of Cub Scouting and the pack, but they're older now and looking forward to more challenging activities. Their uniform is a little different. In fact, they have a choice of uniforms. They can wear either the Cub Scout uniform with Webelos insignia or the Boy Scout uniform with the Webelos insignia.

A little while ago we said that you played a big role in getting Cub Scouts to grow up to be Boy Scouts. Well, the Webelos den is where the challenge is greatest. You can be *the* reason a Webelos Scout becomes a Boy Scout. You'll need to keep in mind that these boys are just one step away from being part of the troop.

Here are some ways you'll be asked to help:

☐ **Assist the Webelos leader as requested.** Webelos leaders are a lot like Webelos Scouts themselves in one way. They expect a lot from a Boy Scout. If you show them what you can do, they'll give you plenty of opportunity to be a leader in the Webelos den.

☐ **Help Webelos Scouts earn activity badges, the Webelos badge, and the Arrow of Light Award.** There are 20 activity badges that Webelos Scouts can earn. They're a little like merit badges, only not quite as involved. You'll want to be familiar with the *Webelos Scout Book* so you will know what is expected.

❑ **Help the denner and assistant denner be leaders.** These guys are like the patrol leader and assistant patrol leader. They are junior leaders in the pack. You can share your leadership experience with them. Use some of the things you learned in your leadership training and make sure they know why.

❑ **Help with the Webelos overnighter.** If there is any area in which the Webelos Scouts are going to look to you for leadership, this is it. You're the Boy Scout. You're expected to know how to camp out. You'll really feel good when you discover how much you know that you can share with the younger boys. Don't restrict your knowledge just to overnighters, either. You can use some of your outdoor skills on hikes and picnics, too.

❑ **Help with Webelos Scout/Boy Scout activities.** Part of your job will involve helping out with activities that the Boy Scouts and the Webelos den do together. For example, when the Webelos den visits a troop meeting, you'll want to get involved early. You know what the Webelos Scouts like and what they can do. So you'll be a key junior leader when it is time to plan for the joint meeting. The same thing is true if the Webelos Scouts are going to camp out with the troop.

❑ **Keep in touch with the assistant Scoutmaster of the new Scout patrol.** The assistant Scoutmaster will know what's happening in the troop that will be of interest to the Webelos Scouts, and you'll know what's happening in the den that should be of interest to the troop. The assistant Scoutmaster will help you prepare for the Webelos Scouts to visit a troop meeting.

❑ **Encourage Webelos Scouts to join the Boy Scouts when they're ready.** This almost goes without saying, doesn't it? Every good Webelos den chief is also a good recruiter for the troop. He can introduce Webelos Scouts to the troop, make the troop leaders aware of who is about to graduate from the den, and generally make it easy and natural for a Webelos Scout to cross the bridge into Boy Scouting.

Here's the
job in a nutshell: **DEN CHIEF**

Job description: The den chief works with the Cub Scouts, Webelos Scouts, and den leaders in the Cub Scout pack.

Reports to: the den leader in the pack and the assistant Scoutmaster for the new Scout patrol in the troop.

Den chief duties:

❑ Knows the purposes of Cub Scouting

❑ Helps Cub Scouts advance through Cub Scout ranks

❑ Encourages Cub Scouts to join a Boy Scout troop upon graduation

❑ Assists with activities in the den meetings

❑ Is a friend to the boys in the den

❑ Helps out at weekly den meetings and monthly pack meetings

❑ Meets with adult members of the den, pack, and troop as necessary

❑ Sets the example

❑ Wears the uniform correctly

❑ Lives by the Scout Oath and Law

❑ Shows Scout spirit

Chapter

Venture: The Fun Is Just Beginning

John Paul Jones, Revolutionary War hero and father of the American Navy, gets credit for the famous saying, "I have not yet begun to fight." It was a statement that rallied sailors of a new, young country to battle and to victory.

So, to paraphrase John Paul Jones: "You have not yet begun to have fun." Oh, you've had fun, all right. But as you grow into the Venture activities in your troop, you'll discover challenges and opportunities that will far outdistance earlier experiences.

As a Venture patrol leader, you'll call upon many skills and experiences of past leadership positions in Boy Scouting. You, as well as the other guys on the Venture patrol or team, are still an important part of the troop. The younger boys need your leadership and example. You will want to keep participating with the rest of the troop in many activities.

Still, you're older now. You're bigger, stronger, smarter, and more adventurous. You find yourself seeking more

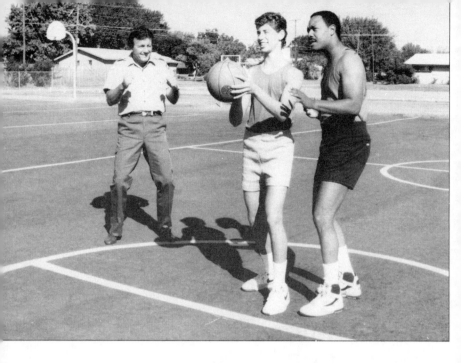

excitement and more rewarding challenges. You joined the Venture patrol, and you're the newly elected patrol leader.

Take a Page from Their Book

Patrol leaders in the troop use many of the same skills you'll use as a Venture patrol leader. Perhaps you were a troop patrol leader and have firsthand knowledge of these skills.

Whether you were a patrol leader or not, you'll find it useful to "take a page from their book." In all honesty, you'll probably use not just one, but several pages.

It would be a good idea to take a peek at these pages right now. Perhaps you should even mark them so you can find them easily in the future. They're full of useful information that you can refer to from time to time.

In chapter 3, you'll find information on such things as elections, troop and patrol organization, appointing assistant leaders, the patrol leaders' council (remember that you're part of this group), planning meetings, advancement, recruiting, and more.

As part of the patrol leaders' council you'll have the opportunity to play an important leadership role in the troop. You'll want to check out chapter 8, so that you're prepared as a member of the patrol leaders' council.

The Venture patrol leader reports to the assistant Scoutmaster for Venture activities. This assistant Scoutmaster serves as an adviser to the group and works closely with the Venture patrol leader in such ways as recruiting program consultants, locating equipment and resources, and arranging for transportation.

The Trail to Eagle Continues

There's no reason for progress along the trail to Eagle to stop (or even slow down), just because you're traveling a different path. Chapter 9 is all about program planning and advancement. It will help you understand how to go about planning your Venture program so that advancement still happens for the members of your group.

Finally, there's a chapter on leadership, relationships, and problem solving. It's chapter 10, and it's full of information that good leaders use all the time. You might want to read chapter 10 with a highlighter pen in your hand so that you can make those points that really hit home stand out. For example, if you're having difficulty with Venture patrol members not understanding your directions, pay particular attention to the information on communication.

It's Up to You

What you make of your leadership role is up to you. Program planning is just as important for Venture patrols as it is for other patrols and the troop. A lot of literature is available on the Venture program. Some of this literature takes the form of activity pamphlets to help you plan. You can get these pamphlets at your BSA local council service center or trading post.

You'll find pamphlets on such activities as backpacking, survival, cycling, freestyle biking, fishing, snow camping, orienteering, mechanics, and whitewater. Other sporting activity pamphlets can help you plan for basketball, volleyball, softball, soccer, tennis, shooting sports, and triathlon.

Ask the Experts

As you begin to get into the activity that you and the other Scouts choose you may need some "expert" advice. The assistant Scoutmaster for the older Scout programs will help you recruit the "experts" you need.

Before you get started though, have everyone make sure he's in good physical condition. You don't want any accidents because someone wasn't up to the rigors of the event. You might even want everyone to get a physical exam. Then, of course, before the big event, you'll want to make sure everyone has the skills necessary to participate and enjoy the activity.

That's what *program* is all about.

Putting Your Stamp on Program

One of the best things about being a leader is that you can be creative with the program. You can explore your ideas and those of the other guys and put your stamp on things.

You may choose to use the program just as it is in the book. Or you may choose to use an entirely different program that members of your Venture patrol suggest. Maybe you'll decide to combine some of your ideas with those you find in an activity pamphlet. The book *Passport to High Adventure* will help with ideas on how to bring your adventure or challenge to life. It's available at your BSA local council service center or trading post.

Leadership Is Leadership

Leadership isn't all that different from one job to another, or from one part of Scouting to another. Leadership is leadership. Still, there are certain rules you'll want to build into your thinking as a junior leader in a Venture patrol.

1. Bring the other members of your patrol into the decision-making process. This is a classic example of where two heads (or five or six or more) are better than one. Let everybody put their ideas on the table so you can explore them together.

2. When you've agreed on the activity you want to explore, discuss it with your assistant Scoutmaster.

3. Ask your assistant Scoutmaster to contact the BSA local council office to ensure that the activity is approved by the Boy Scouts of America. **This is very important!** Before you begin, it's also a good idea to get approval on any ultimate adventure you're planning from the adults connected with your troop; this means the troop committee, parents, and your Scoutmaster. There's no sense in doing all the work

only to find out that you won't be allowed to put it to good use.

4. Recruit the experts. In many ways this will be a familiar experience for you. It's somewhat like contacting a merit badge counselor. The expert you recruit will work with your group to help teach the skills involved. You'll definitely want to use this know-how in planning the meetings leading up to the ultimate adventure. Often it's important that skills are learned in a certain order.

5. When planning your ultimate adventure, use the "Activity Plans" found in the activity pamphlets. It will guide you through all the steps necessary. It will also help you make certain that everyone has a role to play.

6. Now, it's time to put your plan to work. Each week, you'll want to review your progress with your assistant Scoutmaster. It's a good idea to double-check on the planned participation of your "expert." Remember, the expert is a key player in making the ultimate adventure happen. If for some reason, often beyond anyone's control, the expert cannot participate as planned, it's better to know this early, so you can find a substitute or rearrange the schedule to accommodate his participation.

7. Each week you'll learn a new skill or prepare some other important aspect for the big game or the ultimate adventure. While this is going on, you'll want to check on such things as transportation, permits, equipment, and food. Naturally, you'll have these various areas (and perhaps others) assigned to members of your group. All you have to do is check with the other members of the Venture patrol to make certain they have their responsibility well in hand.

Behind Every Good Leader . . .

Few people, if any, ever succeed all by themselves. This is true of presidents, generals, business leaders, Scoutmasters, parents, and Venture patrol leaders.

You really need to put together a team. As we said in an earlier chapter, a team or group is a group of people with common goals.

Let's look at a typical Venture patrol. As patrol leader, you're elected to represent your Venture patrol on the patrol leaders' council. Your term of office will last until the patrol completes its ultimate adventure. Then the Venture patrol will choose a new patrol leader for the next adventure. Your Venture patrol members also expect you to be the spark plug that makes this crew go. They will look to you for ideas. They expect you to be prepared.

Much of the preparation will come from program planning, which is discussed in chapter 9. The ideas, however, are another animal all together. Where do they come from? Many of them will come from the members of your Venture patrol, with your help.

Don't get worried. You're not in this alone any more than the troop patrol leaders are or the senior patrol leader is. You have the other members of the patrol leaders' council, the assistant Scoutmaster, the troop committee, and the Scoutmaster. They're all anxious to give you a hand when you need it.

But that's sort of looking "up the ladder," isn't it? Sometimes the resources available to us that are "up the ladder" seem a little distant. There are other resources available that can be of tremendous help.

Let's look "down the ladder." You'll find some valuable resources among your Venture patrol members. Their enthusiasm, ideas, and skills make you rich in "natural" resources. You'll find more on using your resources in chapter 10.

Here's the job of the **Venture patrol leader**
in a nutshell:

Job description: The Venture patrol leader is the elected leader of his Venture patrol. He represents his patrol on the patrol leaders' council.

Reports to: the assistant Scoutmaster/Venture.

Venture patrol leader duties:

❏ Provides leadership for the selected high-adventure activities or sports

❏ Keeps Venture patrol members informed

❏ Represents the Venture patrol at patrol leaders' council meetings

❏ Encourages Venture patrol members to take part in all troop activities

❏ Locates and secures resources necessary for the Venture patrol activities

❏ Develops Venture patrol spirit and control

❏ Works with other troop leaders to make the troop run well

❏ Sets the example

❏ Wears the uniform correctly

❏ Lives by the Scout Oath and Law

❏ Shows Scout spirit

Chapter 8

The Patrol Leaders' Council Makes It Happen

One early spring night, the air had that fresh, clean smell, and it had warmed to shirtsleeves comfort. Mike, the senior patrol leader, decided to hold the patrol leaders' council meeting outdoors. His dad helped him pull out the picnic table from storage behind the garage. The only thing he had to worry about now was the bugs. In case they were bad, he retrieved the bug repellent from his camping gear.

As the patrol leaders gathered, their anticipation was high. Tonight they'd start getting ready for the district's spring camporee. While winter camping had been exciting, the camporee would be different and the challenge of head-to-head competition with patrols from all over the district was adding to their anticipation.

Patrol leaders Justin and Greg excitedly shared some memories of last year's camporee. Justin's patrol had won the first aid competition and Greg's had received a ribbon for its swinging gateway to their patrol site. They were anxious to get going again.

Another patrol leader was reviewing the first aid requirements for First Class with an assistant Scoutmaster. He wanted to make sure he understood the requirements because a couple of Scouts in his patrol were going to be working on this requirement.

Mike and his assistant senior patrol leader were already at the table, reviewing the plan for the night's meeting. "Everyone really has to get into this meeting," said the assistant senior patrol leader. "We have a ton of stuff to do."

It was a typical patrol leaders' council meeting scene. These meetings always have to cover a lot of ground because there are always so many things going on in the troop. At this meeting, each patrol leader is ready to represent his patrol. Justin, for example, knows his patrol is anxious to defend its title as the first-place patrol in the first aid competition. The guys want him to make sure they know what the competition will cover this year. Greg's patrol wants to know if the spars it used for its gateway last year are still available.

The patrol leaders' council will deal with Justin and Greg's concerns quickly. Just as quickly, new questions and ideas will pop up. By the time the meeting is over, normally about an hour to an hour and a half later, the patrol leaders' council will have answered the patrol leaders' questions, planned the meetings for the next month, and addressed any problems within the troop.

What Is the Patrol Leaders' Council?

Junior leaders make up the patrol leaders' council—the board of directors, so to speak. It's the decision-making team. The patrol leaders' council plans the annual program, then the weekly meetings leading up to the monthly outdoor adventure. In addition to the material found in this chapter, there is a lot of useful information on the importance of proper planning in chapter 9, "Planning Is the Key."

Together, members of the patrol leaders' council address the needs of each patrol and the general problems that involve the patrols and the troop. As a member of the patrol leaders' council, you represent the whole troop. When the patrol leaders' council meets, you get a chance to express your desires (and those of your patrol members).

The Leader of the Patrol Leaders' Council

The senior patrol leader is the top junior leader in the troop. With the advice of the Scoutmaster, he leads the patrol leaders' council and chairs its meetings, usually once each month.

Who Are the Members of the Patrol Leaders' Council?

Naturally, as the leader of the patrol leaders' council, the senior patrol leader is a member. It's easy to see, just by looking at the name of the group—patrol leaders' council—that the patrol leaders should be members. There are others, too. When your troop has a Scout filling any one of the following positions, he is part of the patrol leaders' council:

❑ Senior patrol leader   ❑ Troop guide

❑ Troop patrol leaders   ❑ Venture patrol leader

❑ Assistant senior patrol leader

The troop scribe should attend patrol leaders' council meetings and keep a log of the meeting, even though he doesn't vote. You may also have occasion to involve other troop members filling non-leadership roles in the troop. The assistant senior patrol leader is responsible for training and giving direction to these non-leadership positions: quartermaster, scribe, historian, librarian, instructor, and chaplain aide. He also represents them at the patrol leaders' council meeting.

Let's say the patrol leaders' council is discussing troop equipment needs. You'll want to have the quartermaster involved. If you're planning a program involving pioneering skills and you have an older Scout who really knows his stuff when it comes to pioneering, then you'd want to invite him so you can make use of his special knowledge.

Following the patrol leaders' council meeting, the assistant senior patrol leader meets with the troop members filling these non-leadership positions to keep them informed of decisions affecting them.

You'll Need a Road Map

In one way, the patrol leaders' council meeting isn't any different from any other meeting or activity. You'll need to chart a course so you know what you're going to do and how you're going to go about it. We usually call this a plan or an agenda. A typical agenda might look like this.

The patrol leaders' council is the troop's decision-making team. Members of the patrol leaders' council address the needs of each patrol, as well as the concerns of the whole troop.

Patrol Leaders' Council Agenda

Date: _____

Opening: As chairman, the senior patrol leader opens the meeting. He might want to start with a brief ceremony. He'll call the meeting to order and take a formal roll call. Then the scribe notes who is present and who is not in the log. He then reads the log of the last meeting. It should be short and businesslike. Give everyone the opportunity to comment briefly. The scribe notes any changes agreed upon.

Next the senior patrol leader will ask if anyone will "move" to accept the log as it is (including any changes). This simply means that he needs a voting member of the patrol leaders' council, other than himself, to recommend approval of the log. Any member can "so move." Now he'll ask that someone "second" the "move." This means he's looking for someone else to agree with the person who "moved" the vote. When the "move" is "seconded," he'll ask for the vote. Typically, the log is approved, with only minor notes, if any. The members of the patrol leaders' council show their approval by saying, "Aye." Enter your notes for the opening here.

_____

_____

_____

_____

_____

_____

_____

_____

Patrol Leaders' Reports: The senior patrol leader asks each patrol leader for his "patrol report." Each patrol leader reports on the progress his patrol made since the last meeting. The patrol leader will want to talk about any activities the patrol conducted on its own (maybe it went swimming or held a couple of patrol meetings). The patrol leader will also report on advancement. Enter notes on patrol reports here.

_____

_____

_____

_____

_____

_____

_____

_____

_____

Old Business: When the scribe read the log of the previous patrol leaders' council meeting, everyone noticed that certain items in the log were to be worked on between meetings. For example, maybe the assistant senior patrol leader agreed to find a local expert to accompany the troop on a nature walk and point out edible wild plants. He'll report on progress at this time. Perhaps everyone agreed that the quartermaster should come to the meeting to discuss equipment needs. This is the time for his report. You'll want to discuss anything left undone after the last meeting, during this part of the agenda. Enter notes on old business here.

_____

_____

_____

_____

_____

_____

_____

_____

So far, everything that has taken place is very businesslike. You'll want to try to keep it short and to the point
because the real work is yet to come. That doesn't mean you
want to go over things so fast that you don't do them correctly.
The senior patrol leader will need to keep things moving
right along. Once a point is made, it needs a brief discussion
and a vote. Then move on to the next item on the agenda.

Planning Ahead: The camporee was the big item on the
patrol leaders' council agenda as we began this chapter. This
item could have been a weekend service project, a canoe
trip, or a campout at a nearby park. It really doesn't matter.
At this stage of the meeting, with all the nitty-gritty details
out of the way, the patrol leaders' council directs its attention
to the next month's meetings. These meetings get the troop
ready for 'the month's big event _and_ help every Scout in the
troop progress toward his next rank.

The senior patrol leader will briefly review the program
feature for the month. The patrol leaders already know the
program feature because they selected it during the annual
troop program planning conference. They should be prepared with ideas from their patrol members. Also, they may
have a couple of questions.

Everyone has time to bring up his patrol's suggestions. It's important to make suggestions brief so that everything gets discussed. Then, when everyone knows what the suggestions are, certain suggestions will quickly move to the top of the list. A little more discussion and a vote will decide which suggestions should be worked into the next few meetings.

Enter notes on planning ahead here.

_____

_____

_____

_____

_____

_____

_____

_____

_____

Meeting Planning: Each meeting has to be planned. The Troop Meeting Plan sheets found in *Troop Program Features* make it easy to plan the meetings now that you know what you want to get done. *Troop Program Features* contains all 36 monthly program features and 4 weeks of meeting activities and an outdoor program plan for each program feature. In support of these program features, it also contains vital materials on community service, outdoor program, program specialties, ceremonies, and Scoutmaster's Minutes. *Troop Program Features,* therefore, is your indispensable resource for planning.

Each meeting has seven parts, as follow:

- ❏ Preopening
- ❏ Opening ceremony
- ❏ Skills instruction (tailored for new Scouts, experienced Scouts, and older Scouts)
- ❏ Patrol meetings
- ❏ Interpatrol activity
- ❏ Closing
- ❏ After the meeting

  Enter your notes on meeting planning here.

_____

_____

_____

_____

_____

_____

_____

_____

New Business: This is where business that isn't part of program planning or that was held over from last month gets a chance. Let's say the pastor of a neighborhood church asks for help setting up an antiques show. Respectfully, the troop has to consider the request. A patrol leader might volunteer his patrol, saying, "Most of my guys go to that church. We can help." Also, he might suggest that any other Scout who wants to join him is welcome to do so.

What if the troop cannot honor the pastor's request? This could happen for many reasons. Maybe the antiques show is the same weekend as the big trip the troop has been planning since fall. Someone must get back to the pastor with an explanation and perhaps another suggestion of how the troop might be helpful.

This is the time during each patrol leaders' council meeting when it is really important to speak up. Remember, the only dumb question is an unasked question. The only ideas that cannot work are those we don't share with others.

Enter your ideas for new business here.

_____

_____

_____

_____

_____

The Scoutmaster's Time

We haven't mentioned the Scoutmaster yet, have we? Well, this person has been at the meeting all along. Since things are going in the right direction, the Scoutmaster will just observe. If a question comes up that the patrol leaders' council members cannot answer, the Scoutmaster's there ready to help. If you need a suggestion, it's a good bet he or she will be ready with one. Otherwise, the Scoutmaster really doesn't need to do too much at a patrol leaders' council meeting.

At the end of the meeting though, the senior patrol leader will turn to the Scoutmaster to indicate that the meeting has come to an end. The Scoutmaster is likely to stand up and say something like this: "Well, Mike, I think you and the rest of the patrol leaders' council really have your act together tonight. We're in for an exciting month. Keep in mind as you go along that Scouts in the new-Scout patrol don't have all the skills some of you do. You'll want to be on the lookout for ways to help them. Paul, as the troop guide, don't hesitate to let anybody on the patrol leaders' council or the adult staff know when you think the patrol can use some help. I'd also like to see us get everyone into full uniform for the camporee. That's about it. Good job, Scouts."

Quickie Meetings

Quickie meetings are more than a good idea. They're very important. The senior patrol leader may call a quickie meeting of the patrol leaders' council at any time. Say a problem comes up during a camping trip. It's quickie-meeting time. Maybe a change in the weather means you need to come up with a quick program change. Time for a quickie meeting. Maybe an expert you'd planned to have attend a meeting had to cancel at the last minute. Time for a quickie meeting.

There's also the quickie meeting that the patrol leaders' council holds at the end of each regular troop meeting. This meeting lets you review how things are going, remind your-selves about what you need for the next meeting, and agree on any minor changes in plans that may be needed.

Chapter

Planning Is the Key

Wait a minute! Why are we talking about planning? Why is it such a big deal? Well, you don't begin a trip without knowing where you are going or how you will get there, do you? In fact, you don't want to begin anything important until you have some plan as to what you're doing. As the old saying goes, "Get your ducks in a row" before you get started. In other words, let's make sure we have everything ready before we begin.

That's one reason you're reading this handbook, isn't it? You want to make sure you're prepared to handle your job as a junior leader. Let's use this thought as we look forward to one of the most important tasks you'll take on as a junior leader — planning. What a dull-sounding word. "Planning," you say, "is something Mom does before preparing a big Thanksgiving Day dinner." You're 100 percent correct. And, while it may seem like a boring activity to you, just think about how much you enjoy the dinner.

Planning is also what your favorite musical groups do before they go on tour. The top 20 NCAA basketball and football coaches do a lot of planning before they begin a season or even send the starting lineup out for one game. Outdoors enthusiasts plan before they take to the woods.

Are you starting to get the picture? Planning simply means taking the time to get ready for whatever it is you want to do.

So let's look at the importance of program planning, one of the most important responsibilities you have as a junior leader.

We have to recognize that a well-planned program ensures the excitement will be there. Planning is how we can be certain the Scouts in our patrol or troop develop the skills they need to prepare for adventure and fun. It gives us confidence going into each meeting, event, or activity. We know what's supposed to happen and that everyone is prepared to make it happen.

Whether we're interested in ceremonies, hikes, skill demonstrations, games, or service projects, doesn't make any difference. If we take the time to plan, then we've replaced that uncomfortable feeling of uncertainty with a feeling of confidence. We've taken an activity that could be all jumbled up, confused, and even boring, and assured ourselves that it will run smoothly and will be jam-packed with excitement, fun, adventure, and advancement opportunity.

Planning Resources

Okay, the first thing that we want to look at is what we'll call "planning resources." You're likely to find planning resources in any number of places. You're already familiar with some of these resources, such as this handbook and the *Boy Scout Handbook*. Others, such as *Troop Program Resources, Troop Program Features, Boy Scout Requirements,* and the *Boy Scout Songbook* are likely to be in your troop library. Others, if you don't have them and if they're not in the troop library, may be purchased for yourself or your patrol. These could include merit badge pamphlets, activity pamphlets, and *Boys' Life* magazine issues.

Troop Program Features

You'll want to take the time to get to know these resources. *Troop Program Features,* for example, is a great troop program planning tool. You'll find enough activities to keep you going for years. Each program feature has four meetings already outlined for you that lead up to a monthly outdoor experience. It doesn't make any difference whether you're planning for the troop or the patrol, you'll find that *Troop Program Features* is a great guide. It will help you plan a day or a weekend outdoor activity. It even has games and ceremonies.

Boy Scout Handbook

You don't need to be introduced to the *Boy Scout Handbook.* No doubt you've really become familiar with it as you've worked your way through the ranks. Take another look at it now that you're a junior leader.

From your leadership position you look at things differently. This includes the *Boy Scout Handbook.* You can open it to almost any page and find something to do, can't you? This means you can build a program around almost every page of the book.

Let's see how this can work when you're planning a camping trip. Open it up to page 278. What do you find? Okay, let's plan for cooking in aluminum foil on this trip. Now we'll open the book again. This time, we open to pages 141–47, where we find illustrations of various lashings. So, why not hold a morning skill demonstration on lashings?

Next we happen to open to page 134 and discover collecting evidence of native plants. This can be useful for two parts of our camping trip. In the afternoon, we can spend time hunting for the native plants, and later we can add them to our pressed-leaf collection.

Hey, a plan is starting to come together, isn't it? See how easy it is to use your *Boy Scout Handbook* as a resource? If you really take the time to get familiar with this book, you'll never be at a loss for something to plan into your program.

Troop Program Planning Video

Planning youth troop's program is an exciting opportunity. The *Troop Program Planning* video can help guide the senior patrol leader and Scoutmaster as they plan for the annual program planning conference.

Boys' Life Magazine

You're missing a good thing if you don't subscribe to *Boys' Life*. Not only does it allow you to enjoy Scouting even when you're not actively participating with other Scouts, but it's full of exciting ideas for your patrol and troop. Every month there's something new that you can add to your program and activity ideas.

Who Plans the Program?

It must be obvious by now that Scouting doesn't just happen. It's planned. You've already seen in chapter 3, "The Patrol Leader's Job," that patrol leaders need to plan programs and activities. In chapter 2, "Standing Tall, Up Front," we noted that the senior patrol leader gets involved in planning. Then in chapter 8, "The Patrol Leaders' Council Makes It Happen," you saw that the patrol leaders' council did its share of planning, too.

Your Scoutmaster does a lot of planning. Members of the board of review do some planning. Your patrol's grubmaster plans. In short, everybody plans.

So, What Does a Program Plan Look Like?

How detailed does a program plan have to be? Really, it isn't all that bad. Often you can put the whole plan on one or two sheets of paper. A sample of planning sheets for a month from *Troop Program Features* are included on the next page. You can also find a sample patrol meeting agenda on page 40 in chapter 3. Feel free to use them exactly as you see them.

These are samples, though. Each is just one way to put a program together. You should feel free to make changes so that they will fit your needs.

Hike Plan

The first thing you might want to do is turn to page 199 in the *Boy Scout Handbook*; there you'll discover what you need to be thinking about as you begin to plan your hike. You'll also want to consult the hiking program feature in *Troop Program Features*. Getting ready for your hike may well take a whole month of troop and patrol meetings. These pages will show you many things you need to consider.

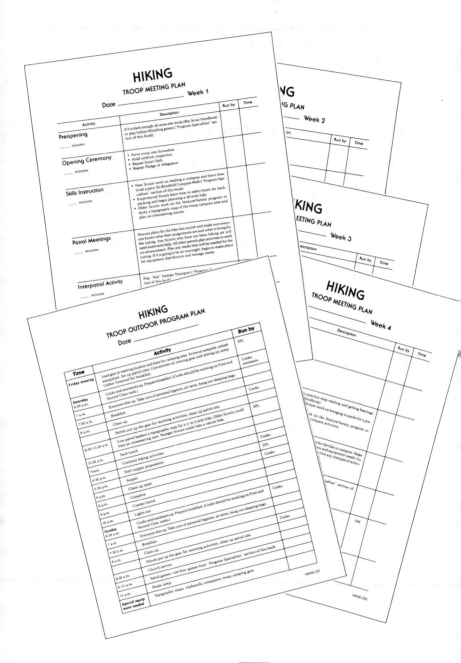

HIKING
TROOP MEETING PLAN
Week 1

Date _____

Activity	Description	Run by	Time
Preopening ___ minutes	If it is dark enough, do some star study (Boy Scout Handbook) or play Indian Wrestling games ("Program Specialties" section of this book).		
Opening Ceremony ___ minutes	• Form troop into horseshoe. • Hold uniform inspection. • Repeat Scout Oath. • Repeat Pledge of Allegiance.		
Skills Instruction ___ minutes	• New Scouts work on reading a compass and learn how to set a pace. Do Blindfold Compass Walk ("Program Specialties" section of this book). • Experienced Scouts learn how to select boots for backpacking and begin planning a 20-mile hike. • Older Scouts work on the Venture/Varsity program or study a topographic map of the troop campout area and plan an orienteering course.		
Patrol Meetings ___ minutes	Discuss plans for the hike this month and make sure everyone knows what their assignments are and what to bring for the outing. Any Scouts who have not been hiking yet will need some extra help. All other patrol plan activities to work on advancement. Plan any meals that will be needed for the outing. If it is going to be an overnight, begin to make plans for equipment distribution and tentage needs.		
Interpatrol Activity ___ minutes	Play "Hot" Isotope Transport ("Program ..." tion of this book)		

HIKING
TROOP OUTDOOR PROGRAM PLAN

Date _____

Time	Activity	Run by
Friday evening	Load gear at meeting location and leave for camping area. Arrive at campsite, unload equipment. Set up patrol sites. Concentrate on stowing gear and setting up camp. Gather firewood for breakfast.	SPL
Saturday 6:30 a.m.	Cooks and assistants up. Prepare breakfast. (Cooks should be working on First and Second Class rank.)	Cooks, assistants
7 a.m.	Everyone else up. Take care of personal hygiene, air tents, hang out sleeping bags.	Cooks
7:30 a.m.	Breakfast	
8 a.m.	Clean up	SPL
	Patrols put up the gear for morning activities, clean up patrol site.	
8:30–11:30 a.m.	Give patrol leaders a topographic map for a 3- to 5-mile hike. Older Scouts could have an orienteering race. Younger Scouts could take a nature hike.	
11:30 a.m.	Sack lunch	Cooks
Noon	Continue hiking activities.	SPL
4:30 p.m.	Start supper preparation.	Cooks
5:30 p.m.	Supper	
6 p.m.	Clean up meal	
8 p.m.	Campfire	Cooks
9 p.m.	Cracker barrel	
10 p.m.	Lights out	
Sunday 6:30 a.m.	Cooks and assistants up. Prepare breakfast. (Cooks should be working on First and Second Class ranks.)	Cooks
7 a.m.	Everyone else up. Take care of personal hygiene, air tents, hang out sleeping bags.	
7:30 a.m.	Breakfast	
8 a.m.	Clean up	
	Patrols put up the gear for morning activities, clean up patrol site.	
8:30 a.m.	Church service	
9–11 a.m.	Patrol games—use four games from "Program Specialties" section of this book.	
11 a.m.	Break camp.	
Special equipment needed	Topographic maps, clipboards, compasses, troop camping gear.	

HIKING 257

HIKING
TROOP MEETING PLAN
Week 2

	Description	Run by	Time

HIKING
TROOP MEETING PLAN
Week 3

	description	Run by	Time

HIKING
TROOP MEETING PLAN
Week 4

	Description	Run by	Time
	...s practice map reading and getting bearings ...Handbook) ...Scouts work on bringing in packs for a pre- ...rk on the Venture/Varsity program or ...compass activities.		
	...s for the hike or campout. Make ...nts and equipment needs. Go ...ection any interpatrol activi...		
	...alties" section of		
		SM	

HIKING 255

Objective: (Why are we going on this hike? How does it fit into the advancement needs of my patrol members?)

_____

_____

_____

_____

Destination: (Where are we going?)

_____

_____

_____

_____

Transportation to and from the trailhead: (How do we get to the starting point? How do we get back home?)

_____

_____

_____

_____

TIME	ACTIVITY	EQUIPMENT NEEDS
7:00 a.m.	Depart for trailhead.	Day packs
7:30 a.m.	Depart from trailhead.	Topographic map/compass
11:00 a.m.	Arrive at Spruce Pond; stop for lunch.	Camera/film
		Trail lunch
		Canteens
		Rain gear
5:00 p.m.	Return to trailhead.	
5:30 p.m.	Arrive home.	

Annual Troop Program Planning Conference

This is really where the whole idea of program planning starts to come together. You and the other junior leaders form the patrol leaders' council. You are the planners for the troop. During the annual program planning conference, usually held in the late summer, the patrol leaders' council gathers to figure out the general program plan for the coming year.

We're not interested at this time in deciding all the little details. All we want to do is set the monthly program features, schedule important dates (such as campouts, summer camp, camporees, etc.), and get everyone off to a good start.

Your Scoutmaster will come to this planning session with the dates for district, council, community, and chartered organization activities. It will be helpful if you have the dates of important holidays, school and church activities, and other occasions that will be competing for the time and attention of your Scouts and their families.

Here Comes the Senior Patrol Leader

As we noted in chapter 8, "The Patrol Leaders' Council Makes It Happen," the senior patrol leader leads the patrol leaders' council. This means he also chairs this planning session. He should have met with the Scoutmaster beforehand to review all five steps of the *Troop Program Planning* video and to discuss any schedule conflicts that might be expected, dates for special activities, Scouts' advancement needs, special events (like courts of honor), monthly program features, etc.

At least a month beforehand, the senior patrol leader should give each member of the patrol leaders' council as much information about the session as possible. The patrol leaders can then share these thoughts with their patrol members. The more ideas included at this time, the better.

When the patrol leaders meet with their patrols, these thoughts and ideas will get the ball rolling. Each Scout should

be encouraged by his patrol leader to add his ideas to the list. Then, as the patrol leader discusses all the ideas with his patrol, he can get a feel for what they'd like to see included in the final plan. The patrol leaders take the new ideas and thoughts to the annual program planning conference.

What's happening here? It's the same thing we talked about in chapter 3 when we noted that the patrol and the troop organizations work just like our government. This is representative government at its best. Everybody, from the newest Scout in the troop right up to the top junior leader, gets his say in things.

The patrol leader gets to represent his part of the community, the patrol. The result should be an annual program with something that everyone can be excited about.

The *Troop Program Planning* video is the guide for the annual program planning conference. This video contains all the basic information for planning the troop's annual and monthly program. *Troop Program Features* and *Troop Program Resources* are the only other principal pieces of literature needed for this session. The next four pages contain the agenda for an annual program planning conference included in the planning video.

The Troop Program Planning Conference

No time limits have been placed on the conference agenda, but working sessions should last no longer than forty-five minutes before a break.

Opening activity: The Scoutmaster conducts an "all aboard" activity, which fosters a spirit of working together to solve a common problem.

Conference objectives and ground rules: The senior patrol leader writes these conference objectives where everyone can see them:

❑ Decide on our troop's goals for the coming year.

❑ Develop a troop program that represents ideas received from the entire troop.

The senior patrol leader reviews these ground rules:

❑ The senior patrol leader presides.

❑ Each event and program will be voted on.

❑ The majority rules.

Video: The senior patrol leader introduces the video, saying something like this: "The video you are about to see should give you a pretty good idea why we have this conference and what we need to accomplish today."

Show part 2 of the *Troop Program Planning* video.

The senior patrol leader continues: "As you saw in the video, we have already completed a couple of items on the annual planning conference agenda. Do you have any questions about what we need to do for the balance of the day?"

Troop goals: The Scoutmaster leads a discussion on troop goals for the coming year in such areas as advancement, service, or troop money-earning projects. (These would be the same goals discussed earlier with the troop committee and senior patrol leader.)

The patrol leaders' council determines the goals by voting on each one.

Major events: The senior patrol leader lists major events the troop could participate in:

❑ Scout shows

❑ Camporees

❑ Summer camp

❑ Special troop events

❑ Good Turn

❑ Patrol suggestions for special activities

The group votes on each event. The senior patrol leader (or designated helpers) deletes activities from the calendar that the troop will not participate in, inserts the events on a clean copy of the Troop Planning Worksheet, and backdates the necessary preparation time into the troop calendar for each event.

Game break: The senior patrol leader might say, "We've been using our 'mind muscles' for awhile, so let's play a fun game." He asks a patrol leader to pick a game from *Troop Program Resources*, then lead it.

Patrol suggestions for program features: The senior patrol leader leads a discussion on the program features to be used for the coming year:

❑ Will they meet the goals of the troop?

❑ What are the advancement opportunities?

❑ Where do they best fit into the calendar?

The group votes on each program feature, then inserts the selected ones on the Troop Planning Worksheet.

Lunch or game break: If lunch is served, make sure it is easy to prepare or that someone other than the patrol leaders' council is responsible. If a game is played, the senior patrol leader selects an action game from *Troop Program Resources*.

Special troop activities: The senior patrol leader presides in deciding on a schedule for the following activities:

❑ Boards of review

❑ Courts of honor

❑ Recruitment nights

❑ Webelos Scout graduation

Add these dates to the Troop Planning Worksheet.

Troop planning worksheet: The senior patrol leader puts this worksheet in final form for presentation to the troop committee.

Game break: Select an activity with the purpose of reflecting on how planning, teamwork, and good communication skills are needed in a good troop program.

Here are some questions to get you started:

❑ What do you think is the purpose of this activity?

❑ How were group decisions made in completing this activity?

❑ Was the plan well communicated? If not, what were the problems?

❑ How did cooperative behavior lead to completing the activity successfully?

❑ How can we use this experience in implementing our troop program?

Monthly program planning: The last step in planning is to plan in detail one month's program for the troop. The video will describe how this is accomplished.

> **Show part 3 of the *Troop Program Planning* video.**

The senior patrol leader says, "We have chosen (name of program feature) for next month's troop program." He distributes copies of pages from *Troop Program Features* related to this program feature or, if copies are unavailable, blank copies of the troop meeting plan.

Even if the troop is very experienced, for today, use *Troop Program Features* as written. Plan the monthly highlight event first. Then plan the troop meetings. Have patrols volunteer for different parts of the meetings. Week 1 in *Troop Program Features* is usually pretty detailed, but in the following weeks the group may need to select ideas from the resource sections in *Troop Program Resources*.

Scoutmaster's comments: Congratulate the Scouts on planning a good troop program. Explain that the plan will not be final until the troop committee is sure they can support everything the patrol leaders' council wants to do. They may have to compromise, but if so, the senior patrol leader will review the issues with them before they vote on the recommendations. Once this is done, plan a parents' night to introduce the year's program to the Scouts and their parents.

Your vote counts. When all the ideas have been discussed, all the best dates have been looked at, and everyone has the information he needs to make decisions, then and only then is it time to vote.

You'll want to keep in mind that you're representing others in your troop. This means that you'll keep their needs in mind and not vote just for those things that you like best. Your job at this point is to use your knowledge of Scouting, your experience, and your understanding of the individual needs of each Scout to build a plan for the year that works for everyone. Everyone gets the opportunity to advance. Everyone has fun.

Put it on a calendar. Once the patrol leaders' council has done its best, it will put the plan on a calendar and get the final approval of the troop committee. With this "seal of approval," it's time to distribute the calendar to the Scouts and their parents. Now everyone can start to get excited about the upcoming year.

With the Troop Planning Worksheet filled out and the calendar completed, the yearly plan is set. The details of each monthly program will be worked out at patrol leaders' council meetings during the year.

Routine events and activities seldom need more than a month to prepare. So, the regular patrol leaders' council meeting is the place to make those final decisions. Don't forget the resources we talked about earlier, especially *Boys' Life.* It will have some of the most up-to-date ideas you can find.

If you haven't read chapter 8, "The Patrol Leaders' Council Makes It Happen," now is a good time to look at it. It will give you a much better idea of how the patrol leaders' council plans each month's activities.

Every 3 months the patrol leaders' council should review the annual plan to see how things are really going. You may need to make some adjustments. Or you may want to make a note for next year's troop program planning conference because one thing you tried worked exceptionally well, or because it didn't. Often the changes required are simply because the circumstances changed.

A big event in your hometown, an illness of one of your key leaders, a storm that causes you to cancel an activity, or any number of other things can affect your plans. It's sort of like jamming a stick in your bicycle spokes; you would have to make some adjustments before you could continue on your way. After you had made the adjustments, you'd be back on the road. That's the way it is when something doesn't happen the way you planned for the troop. The patrol leaders' council takes the time to make some adjustments and the program is put back on course.

Planning Troop Meetings

When everything else about program planning is done, particularly the annual troop program planning conference, planning the weekly troop meetings becomes simple.

The Troop Meeting Plan, found in *Troop Program Features,* will take you through every part of a good meeting. The programs outlined in *Troop Program Features* are complete, and you might choose to take advantage of them often.

What's left? Well, at the monthly patrol leaders' council meeting, you'll want to decide who's responsible for each part of the weekly meetings. The patrol leaders' council discusses each part of the meeting so that everyone has a good idea of what they need to do to be prepared. For each activity, a list of equipment and supplies needs to be developed. Who's going to bring the needed supplies? Who's going to check with the quartermaster to check out equipment? Which patrol is going to conduct a demonstration or lead a game?

Remember, you have a limited amount of time for each meeting, usually about 90 minutes from opening ceremony to closing ceremony. A good plan, with everyone understanding it, will ensure that your meetings are better than ever. You'll love it when a good meeting comes off just the way you planned it.

Finally, someone should see to it that all the junior leaders and the adult leaders have copies of the plan you've agreed upon. When each patrol leader gets back to his patrol, he'll want to review the plan with the Scouts. He'll discuss what's going to take place and start getting his patrol ready for their part in making Scouting happen.

Chapter 10

Leadership Begins with a Question

Are you good at keeping a secret? Let's hope not, at least in this case, because one important key to good leadership is a good question. Unfortunately, that's probably one of the best-kept secrets in the world. So let's see to it that every junior leader is in on the secret.

How did that last paragraph begin? With a question, right? What did that question do? It led you into the next statement. "Now, wait a minute," you say. "You can't trick me that way. I didn't *have* to read the next statement." Well, that's true. You didn't have to. But you did read it, didn't you?

Now, it's not a leader's job to get people to do things they don't want to do. Not at all. A good leader gets things done by respecting others and helping them learn and grow through their own Scouting experiences. He provides direct, hands-on leadership when he has to, but always with respect toward others as a guiding force.

Let's take a quick look at how this will work every time. Say you need some help with the opening flag ceremony for the next meeting. Jim, one of the Scouts in your patrol, wants to earn his Tenderfoot rank. If you're on top of things as a leader, you'll know this. Because you know he wants to complete Tenderfoot requirements, you can show him how working with you on the ceremony will help him in his advancement.

You know Jim will be anxious to help because he wants to earn Tenderfoot. So when you ask him to come to the next meeting a little early to get ready for the opening flag ceremony, he will jump at the chance. Now, that was a pretty simple example. But you can start to see how this works.

As important as a good question is, it's certainly not all you need to know to be a good leader. Leadership is about relationships, problem solving, and achieving goals. One skill isn't going to make you a good leader.

Each time you add a new leadership skill though, you become a better leader. On a scale of 1 to 5, you need all

the skills to be a 5. Any skill you lack makes you that much less of a leader. So if all you can do is ask questions, you probably have some work to do.

Let's look at some other leadership skills you might want to add to those you already have.

COMMUNCIATION has to be one of the more important. You might think of this as the ability to get *and* give information. If you communicate in such a way that people understand what you need and why you need it, they respond the way you want them to.

Suppose you had "ordered" Jim to help you with the flag ceremony mentioned previously. Do you think he might have asked himself, "Why is he telling me to do this?" But by showing him how helping with the flag ceremony will help him with his advancement, Jim sees how he will benefit.

So Jim feels like a winner. But so are you as a leader. You can always tell if you are communicating well. If you're getting the response you want, you're doing a good job of getting and giving information. If you're not getting the response you want, watch out.

There are many skills to communicating. We've all seen how the "magic words" work. A "please" or a "thanks" is always a good idea. Using "we" or "ours" will do much more toward your leadership success than "I" or "me."

Give a sincere smile. It's interesting—no matter how many smiles you give away, you never run out. Maybe it's because every time you give someone a smile, they give you one right back. And, did you ever notice how hard it is to stay mad at someone when you're smiling? It's nearly impossible.

How about a good laugh? That works every time, too, especially if you're laughing at yourself. We all make mistakes, and if the Scouts in your patrol see that you recognize your mistakes with a laugh, they'll be quick to forget them.

There is the story about the patrol leader who forgot to bring the snacks for after the campfire. What did he do? He fell on the ground moaning loudly, "Former mental giant drops dead." Then he got to work trying to see how he could save the night. Keep in mind, though, that this kind of quip works well on yourself. Try using it on someone else, and they might feel hurt.

The First Thing You Do Is Agree

When someone says he doesn't want to work on the tower you're building because it's a lot of work, don't argue. Agree with him. Try responding this way: "You're right, John. It is a lot of work. That's what the guys in the Roadrunner Patrol thought last month when they first started their tower. But once they got into it, they found out it was a ton of fun."

This is called the "feel, felt, found" method of leadership. I understand how you *feel*. Others have *felt* the same way. But when they tried it, they *found* that...

There are several important things happening here. First, by agreeing with John, you've stopped the argument. You agreed with him, so there's no one for him to argue with. Then, you further tell him that others felt the same way when they first started their tower. This tells him he's not some kind of dummy for thinking the way he does. Now John is listening to you rather than arguing with you. You're speaking his language. So, it's time to let him in on what other Scouts discovered when they gave it a try. You'll win him over when he sees how much fun they've been having ever since. What does John have to lose by trying, right?

Check Your Toolbox

You wouldn't start a building project without checking to make sure you had all the tools you need, would you? Well, the same thing is true as you set out to lead the Scouts in your patrol or troop. Check your toolbox. This is another way of saying that you should make sure you know what resources are available to you.

While a carpenter will want to have a hammer, saw, some lumber, and other materials, you'll want to have certain things, too. Earlier we talked about using the *Boy Scout Handbook*. It's definitely a tool for any Scouting leader. There are many such resources. We've mentioned them frequently throughout this handbook: *Troop Program Features, Troop Program Resources, Boys' Life,* merit badge pamphlets, activity pamphlets, and many more.

What about people? Don't forget the guys in your patrol. They're a great resource. They have Scouting skills you can use. They also have other skills and knowledge. Perhaps one of the Scouts plays the guitar. Maybe another is really into chemistry. Can you think of ways to use these resources?

Maybe one of their families has some land the patrol can camp on. That's a resource. Maybe a mom or dad is a fire fighter. That's a resource when someone in the patrol wants to work on Fire Safety merit badge. The Troop Resource Survey sheet is a valuable tool for troop leaders who want to find out in which areas of the troop program the parents of troop members may be willing to assist.

Take time right now to list resources. Ask other patrol leaders for their ideas. Check the troop library. Think about people you know and what they do for a living or for fun. How can you work their skill into a patrol or troop activity? Don't be surprised at how many different resources you discover.

Make a game out of it. See which member of the patrol leaders' council can come up with the longest list. You might even want to make a patrol contest out of developing the list. Then, share your list with the other junior leaders. The more resources you develop, the more fun you're going to have in Scouting.

You can keep your list of resources right here.

_____

_____

_____

_____

_____

_____

_____

_____

Help Others Succeed

Almost everything you want to do as a junior leader requires help from someone. Keep in mind how important it is to your success that you help other people be successful.

Here's a game that illustrates what we're saying. Look at some typical needs of a junior leader, in column I. Match them with the typical needs of a Scout, in column II. Draw a line between each item that matches. For example, item A in column I matches with item 7 in column II. ➡

You need to start the camp stove. Because Dan has everything he needs for Second Class except requirement 2f, he needs to build a fire. By asking him to build the fire, you're helping him complete the requirement. He'll be eager to help you get the fire built.

There may be more than one correct set of matches. See one correct set on page 124.

Seeing Needs

As you can see, leadership is almost easy if you learn to match needs. You can easily see from the above examples that understanding what your patrol or troop needs (or wants) is important. This is true for each individual, too.

But you can't help someone get what he needs (or wants) if you don't know what it is. If your troop or patrol keeps an advancement chart on the wall, you'll want to study it regularly. See what each Scout needs to do. Sometimes, just by paying attention, you'll notice what each Scout is eager to do. It may be something he needs for advancement or maybe it is just something he likes doing. Knowing what it is helps you lead.

COLUMN I

A. You need a fire built.

B. Supper has to be prepared, and the cook is late getting back from a hike.

C. First aid skills need to be taught.

D. Rope used for last month's knot-tying demonstration was cut rather than untied as it should have been.

E. Your patrol needs someone to explain symbols on the map for this month's patrol hike.

F. Someone needs to take notes at a patrol meeting.

G. Your patrol isn't paying attention to the task at hand.

COLUMN II

1. A Tenderfoot Scout is working on Second Class. One of the older Scouts has been teaching him first aid, and he's ready to pass requirement 12b.

2. A Second Class Scout cooked breakfast and lunch on the last trip.

3. Kevin went on the last camping trip and learned to orient a map.

4. One Scout in your patrol wants to be considered for a troop office.

5. A new Scout is just starting to work on Tenderfoot.

6. The Roadrunners have challenged your patrol to a game of Capture the Flag.

7. Dan has everything he needs for Second Class except requirement 2f.

A matches with 7: Second Class requirement 2f includes lighting a camp stove. By helping out here, Dan continues working on his advancement.

B matches with 2: Jim cooked breakfast and lunch on the last camping trip. It's a safe bet that he'll want to try again this time around to practice on requirement 4e for First Class, which involves cooking the patrol meals on a camping trip. By cooking, as you need him to, he's able to get what he wants, too.

C matches with 1: Second Class Requirement 6c says, "Demonstrate first aid . . . ." What better way to demonstrate than by teaching a skill to new Scouts. You help the Scout complete the requirement he needs, and he helps you get other Scouts started on their first aid.

D matches with 5: It's too bad the rope has been cut when it should have been untied. Still, the ends of the rope need to be whipped, before they fray. One of the first things a Scout needs to do for Tenderfoot is demonstrate that he can whip a rope.

Are you beginning to see how this works? This Scout is going to be anxious to get the chance to whip a rope. You need to have the rope whipped before it becomes a mess. By asking him to whip the rope, you're helping him get what he wants. By whipping the rope, he's helping you get what you want.

E matches with 3: There's a good chance that if Kevin just learned how to orient a map, he has not drawn a map for a hike yet. He needs to draw a map for Second Class requirement 1a. You need a map if you're taking the patrol on a hike. You're helping him, and he's helping you.

F matches with 4: Taking the notes at the patrol meeting is the job of the patrol scribe. It will give the Scout who wants a troop leadership job a chance to show that he can handle one. And again, you get something done that you need to have done.

G matches with 6: There won't be time for a game of Capture the Flag if the guys don't pay attention to business. Ask them to pay attention so you can get everything done and get to the game. They want to play the game, so chances are they will knuckle down to business as you suggest. Everyone wins.

How to Share Leadership

Often a new leader gets frustrated because he tries to make all the decisions himself. Once he recognizes that others can help, his job becomes much easier.

This is because he starts to share his leadership. Review the section on "Sharing Leadership" in chapter 3, "The Patrol Leader's Job." You might ask, "How do I share leadership?" Well, look at the patrol leader's role as a member of the patrol leaders' council. It's a great example of sharing leadership. The senior patrol leader shares his leadership with all the patrol leaders by assigning different responsibilities to them.

Sharing your job with others makes the task easier.

By discussing things with the members of their patrols, the patrol leaders share their leadership. Each Scout gets to voice his opinion. This way the plan that comes out of the patrol leaders' council meeting will incorporate the thoughts and ideas of the rest of the troop. Because the patrol leader and the senior patrol leader shared their leadership with others, everyone will be more anxious to support the plan and make the plan happen.

When we discussed the jobs of the patrol leader and the senior patrol leader, we also pointed out that there were many other jobs in the troop. As a good leader, you will allow those assigned to other jobs to do them — their way. You may want to check on the job to make certain that it's getting done. You may even want to help train the Scout who has the job. But you won't do it yourself.

Once you share your leadership with someone by asking him to do a certain job, remember that the job is his now, not yours. Stepping in to do it yourself is the same as saying, "Hey, I don't trust you to do the job I asked you to do." That doesn't mean you shouldn't check on things. If you've asked someone to get firewood for the supper fire, it needs to be done on time. You'll want to make sure he starts soon enough and if he hasn't, encourage him to get started: "Say, Jim, we need to start cooking in a few minutes. How's the firewood coming?"

If a couple of the guys are going to get together and plan a patrol hike for next week, it's a good idea to give them a call to see how it's coming along. Until you discover that it's coming along just fine, you may want to call every day.

There's an old saying, "You have to *in*spect what you *ex*pect." This means you need to let people know that once they've accepted an assignment they're not going to be able to slide by without completing it. It's up to you to help the other Scouts in your patrol be successful.

Sharing leadership and ideas makes the troop plan come together.

Listen Closely

Taking the time to listen closely to what people say is one way to share your leadership. The other Scouts will like it when you listen to their ideas. It tells them you care. It shows them you think their ideas are important.

When a leader isn't listening to those he's trying to lead, he really doesn't know if they're following. Pretty soon he's trying to understand why everyone is always grumbling.

Why are the guys unhappy? Why did someone drop out? Often the answer is that they didn't feel they were part

of the action. Nobody cared about their thoughts or feelings.
In this case the "nobody" could be you.

Look Back Once in a While

Sometimes you can get a better look at how well things
are going by taking the time to look at how well they went.
If you want your patrol to be ready for the big fall camporee, you have a lot to get together, to learn, and to practice.
During the patrol leaders' council meeting, you planned
activities that would help you get prepared for the challenge.
When you got back to the patrol, you shared the plan with
everybody in the patrol.

Now, a couple weeks have passed. It's a good idea to
look back at what you thought you were doing. Are you
really getting ready for the camporee? Maybe part of a previous meeting went longer than expected. This meant that you
couldn't practice orienting a map as you had planned. You
still need the skill at the camporee, so you'll want to make
some adjustments during the next couple of weeks to get the
practice you need.

You'll want to take these quick looks back for other reasons, too. Each time you look back at what you've done in
the past few weeks, you'll want to make sure everyone is getting the chance to advance and have a good time.

When you look back, you might discover that one of
the guys hasn't been at two of the last three meetings. Maybe
he's losing interest because the things he thought the troop
was going to do didn't happen. Maybe he's not having fun
because he doesn't know the skills that everyone else is taking
for granted. As a leader, you'll want to pick up on this situation quickly before you lose a member of your group.

Do It Your Way? Sure!

As you can see, there are a lot of things for a leader to
do. Each leader is going to do these things a little bit different from another leader. And that's okay. Still, there is one

thing that every junior leader in the troop will want to do: *Set the example!*

You probably noticed that this thought is part of every job description in this handbook. That's because it is so important. Often the Scouts you lead will learn most of what they know about Scouting from you and your example.

You are their model of what a Scout is. Your ideals will become their ideals. Your skills will be passed along to them. If it looks like you think you can do things in a sloppy fashion, the other Scouts will soon think they can, too. If you're always walking around thinking that your plan won't work, that's what they will think. If you're enthusiastic, they will be enthusiastic.

Earning Respect

When you first become a junior leader, there are certain things that are likely to happen. After everyone has congratulated you, someone is likely to try to see if he can get some special attention from the new leader.

Perhaps he is a good friend and all he wants is to get out of doing dishes, "just this once." You know it's his turn, but he's a good friend; you enjoy his friendship, and you want to keep it that way.

Look what happens if you give in to this request. First, you're going to feel bad. You knew it really wasn't the right thing to do, but you did it anyway. Then you're going to have to get someone else to do a job that's not really his. He's going to be unhappy because you played favorites.

Then, tomorrow, when you need to have your friend gather firewood, he's going to expect that he can beg off "just this once" again. He's not respecting you as a leader or a friend. He's using you selfishly.

Okay, you say he won't ask for a favor again. Maybe he won't, but how do you respond when someone else doesn't want to do their job? Can you really let everyone off easy? Of course not. So it's best to do what you know is right from the very start.

Saying No Is Never Easy

Even though it isn't easy to say no, this doesn't excuse you from doing so when necessary. No one likes to say no, especially to a friend. Still, if that's the correct response, it's what a good leader will say.

"No, we can't take the canoes out." "No, we can't eat the campfire snacks this afternoon." "No, we can't go wading by the waterfall." Every one of these situations might be perfectly all right at the proper time, under the right conditions. But if it's not the right time or the conditions aren't correct, it's time for the leader to really lead.

"Bill, you shouldn't make fun of Mike when he stutters. Mike doesn't stutter because he wants to, you know. Besides, he's part of our patrol, and we don't treat each other that way, okay?" In this case, that's all you have to say. The message is delivered.

Here Comes Real Trouble

Occasionally a troop or patrol will discover that it has a real "wise guy" who is always causing trouble. This isn't the guy who likes to toss in a joke once in a while. It isn't the Scout who moans and groans when it's his turn to gather firewood. The troublemaker is the guy who constantly pushes the younger Scouts around. Maybe he thinks it's okay to always argue with the patrol leader or to make fun of everyone else's opinions. Chances are that this is also the guy who always says, "No," and doesn't want to do much of anything.

It won't be easy to take action. Other Scouts may laugh at his antics. If you read their laughs to mean they like having every meeting interrupted, you are wrong. It won't be easy, but in the interest of your troop or patrol, you will have to take action. If you want the others to follow your leadership, they're going to need to see that you can take care of the tough jobs as well as the easy ones.

Fortunately, we don't run into much "real trouble" in Scouting. The guys who join Scouting know up front what the Scout Oath and Law are all about. They're not joining because they are looking for trouble. Still, it can happen that you get faced with someone accused of stealing, smoking, cheating, taking drugs, or another serious action that is very wrong. You can't let it pass. You *must* take a stand.

If you don't, you'll always know you should have, and it will bother you a lot. Even more important, what will happen to your ability to lead? The other guys are going to see that you walked away from a serious problem, rather than facing it the way a leader should. Whatever respect you've earned up to that point will quickly disappear. They will see that you don't have the courage to do what you know is right.

What do you do? The answer to this question is tough. The action to take won't always be the same. Still, there are certain things you will want to do just about every time.

Begin by taking a good, hard look at the facts. Be as certain as you can that you know what really has happened.

❏ Be certain that the problem is real. Does he admit it? If not, who's making the charges? Do you really believe the charges are true? What is the proof?

❏ Try to give the accused Scout the benefit of the doubt. Did he know what he did was wrong? If not, explain why the action can't take place again. Get a commitment from him not to do it again. Make sure that he knows what action you'll take if it does happen again.

❏ Maybe he says he doesn't like a certain rule. Let him explain while you listen carefully. Try to understand what he's saying and why he feels this way. Then explain why the rule exists and why it's important that everyone in the patrol or troop do their best to obey the rule. Maybe you'll convince him. Remember to use the "feel, felt, found" method.

❏ If he won't agree to follow the rule, or if he breaks the rule again, consult with the senior patrol leader. It may be necessary to bring the Scoutmaster or assistant Scoutmaster into the situation.

❏ If the problem is something really serious, such as using drugs, you don't have many choices. Naturally, you'll want to be absolutely positive that you have the facts. If you think the problem exists, you have to bring it to the attention of someone who can handle it. At the very least, talk to your senior patrol leader about your concerns. He may well recommend that the Scoutmaster be brought in.

Hopefully the Scout who is causing the problem will do what is right when you face up to him. But be careful not to spill all the details to everyone you see. It's no one else's business. If the problem is really serious, though, everything changes. If the police have to become involved or someone is hurt, you're going to want to give information to those in authority who have a right to know all the details.

Remember this—you're not all alone. If you have a problem that's too hot for you to handle, use your resources. Maybe the other guys in the patrol can help. Again, you may want to confide in the senior patrol leader. And you may need to discuss your decision with your Scoutmaster.

Problem or Opportunity?

If you can learn to view problems as opportunities, you will be well on your way to success as a leader. Don't look at every meeting or activity as being littered with problems. View them as activities filled with opportunities.

You can't demonstrate your leadership skills if you never get the opportunity. Does that mean you want people to argue? No, of course not. But when it happens, and it happens in the best troops and patrols, you have the opportunity to lead.

What do you do when an argument arises? It's often best to make light of it. Step between the two who are arguing, even if it's about to get a little physical, and say something like, "Okay, guys, this round is over. Let's get onto something really important." It may be a good idea to keep the two apart for a bit, at least until they cool down. You'll probably find that they're best of friends a short while later.

Of course every leader, good or not so good, will get his share of criticism. You might want to think of it as the spice of leadership. After all, the right spice can turn a humdrum meal into something special. So, if you're getting *honest* and *accurate* criticism, you will want to be thankful. Criticism should help make you a better leader.

If you're getting *heavily* peppered with criticism, there may be a problem. You need to ask yourself why. Maybe you need to ask another junior leader or an adult leader for help. But you don't want to object to useful criticism. Without it you might never know that something needs changing.

If the criticism is unfair, you have another kind of opportunity. Most likely your critic thinks he is being very fair. You're going to have to find out why. This is where the questions we talked about earlier can come into play again. Ask many questions. Find out why he feels this way. Let him talk while you listen closely. If you discover, while listening, that there is some truth to the criticism, address it positively. You'll be a better leader because of it. Perhaps you can enlist the Scout's assistance in solving the problem. Both of you will grow as a result.

What if the criticism is off base? There's a good chance that as the other Scout explains his position, he will discover for himself that he is mistaken. Because he made the discovery himself, it will be a lot easier for him to handle.

Index

O

P

Acknowledgment

The manuscript for this *Junior Leader Handbook* was written by Thomas M. Dwyer, former senior editor of *Boys' Life* and an active Scoutmaster in Syracuse, N.Y.

Notes